MW01256218

SOLID SOULS

SOLID SOULS

Arthur Jones

invite PRESS

Plano, Texas

SOLID SOULS

20 21 22 23 24 25 26 27 28 29 –10 9 8 7 6 5 4 3 2 1

MANUFACTURED IN THE UNITED STATES OF AMERICA

Soul in Hebrew (נֶפֶשׁ) Nephesh — Can mean soul, breath, spirit, personality, life, mood/state of mind, throat/neck.

And the LORD God formed man of the dust of the ground
and breathed into his nostrils the breath of life; and man became a living
soul [נֶפֶשׁ].

Genesis 2:7 KJV

Soul in Greek (ψυχή) Psuke — Can mean life, soul, desire, breath.

For what is a man profited, if he shall gain the whole world,
and lose his own soul? or what shall a man give in exchange
for his soul [ψυχή]?

Matthew 16:26 KJV

And I saw thrones, and they sat upon them, and judgment was given
unto them: and I saw the souls [ψυχή] of them that were beheaded for the
witness of Jesus, and for the word of God, and which had not worshiped
the beast, neither his image, neither had received his mark upon their
foreheads, or in their hands; and they lived and reigned with Christ a
thousand years.

Revelation 20:4 KJV

Contents

This book is dedicated to:

my wife, Becky, who has bound her soul to mine
and has allowed me to bind mine to hers;

&

my children, Ella Reece and Sam, who have taught me
as infants that they have full-sized souls.

They remind me every day to choose a more solid soul.

SOLID SOULS

Preface

Outside of Scripture, C. S. Lewis's *The Great Divorce* has been the most influential book of my life. Lewis's eye-opening allegory on heaven and hell has reshaped how I view myself, my family, my friends, and my life. The book, with its thought-provoking depiction of human choices and desires, made me realize that I, too, make choices every day between heaven and hell without even knowing it. Heaven and hell seem too remote and spiritual to impact our day-to-day lives, but all of us make eternal choices every single day that will determine our future, our relationships, and our well-being.

I hope you will see through this book that the idea of heaven and hell as existing in a remote or distant future is not simply wrong; it is dangerous. The choice between heaven and hell is constantly before us because we live in a world created by a God who gave us the ability to make decisions for our lives. These decisions lead us toward or away from heaven, toward or away from an abundant life. As a pastor, I've realized that it is almost impossible to fully imagine what this means for our daily lives, our families, our work, or our friends. We imagine that salvation is simply an acceptance or rejection of God, but we ignore that such a decision is lived out in the mundane ways we worry, budget, parent, marry, work, and live. These ordinary things reflect pieces of our souls.

You are a soul. You do not *have* a soul, but you *are* a soul. The soul is what lives on after death and everything that you are lives on. Your soul is not some spiritualized vapor or shadow of your existence, but rather the fullness of you. You carry with you into eternity the baggage and benefits of every single decision that you have made. If you consistently make bitter and angry decisions in life, you don't automatically become sweet and charitable after you die.

If you consistently choose to love your enemies and pray for those who persecute you, then guess what? Jesus will say, "Well done, my good and faithful servant" (see Matthew 25:21).

Your choices define you. Your core decisions comprise the totality of your life and reveal who you are in your relationships, direction, and purpose. These are more easily understood as your soul. Some souls are more solid than others. They have integrity and strength. They are unified in purpose and aligned with good, solid virtues. Other souls are fragmented, weak, and shriveled. They are pulled in too many different directions with no alignment of purpose. When we think about the entirety of our lives, we all want to have *solid souls* that are filled with meaning and purpose. We need, therefore, to think more deeply about the choices we make and figure out how our souls can thrive and become more solid. All that we do either adds to or detracts from the quality of our souls. As Jesus preached and Lewis wrote, whether we experience heaven now and forevermore is wrapped up in what we believe, the choices we make, and who we are each and every day.

I am not an expert on what I consider to be Lewis's greatest book, and I do not claim to be a fit heir to so great a genius. But I have seen the truth of this story lived out in my life and in the pages of Scripture through the teachings of Jesus. And I will claim to be on my own intentional trajectory of seeking a more solid soul. In dedicating my life to seeking heaven, I hope I can help you see that your every choice leads you closer or further away from your eternal destination.

Let's thrive as solid souls together,
Arthur Jones
Dallas, TX 12/25/2020

Soul

The entire eternal substance that encompasses every part of a person: physical body, spirit, and personality.

Solid Soul

A fully integrated person—body, spirit, personality—who continuously makes choices that move himself or herself toward heaven.

Shriveled Soul

A diminished person, who constantly makes choices to benefit one's own self, eventually resulting in hell.

Introduction | Solidify Your Soul

Cradling Life

My wife Becky and I journeyed down the long and often relentless road of infertility for several years. By God's grace, we were given the gift of a son, Sam, in 2017. Twenty-three short months later, we introduced him to his little sister Ella Reece. Twice now, I have had the privilege of witnessing the birth of a tiny, screaming, messy, beautiful, healthy baby.

Through both pregnancies, countless people warned me about the seismic shift that would take place in my life. These comments, though well intentioned, were rarely helpful. During our first pregnancy, the warnings sounded like this:

> "Are you ready for your life to change?"
> "Have you gotten enough sleep?"
> "Don't blink!"
> And most unhelpfully: "You have no idea what is coming your way."

This final comment was mildly frustrating simply because it was so obvious. I had never been a dad. How in the world could I know what was coming my way? No one does. But the second time around, it took a different tone because our second happened to be a little girl:

> "She is going to have you wrapped around her finger!"
> "Watch out! You won't be able to say no!"

Each of these comments was well intended but ultimately rung hollow next to the experience of holding my child. At each birth, the baby was placed almost immediately with my wife for some bonding time. After a few minutes, a nurse took the baby for weighing and cleaning, and then handed the baby to me to cradle in my arms. These two moments are permanent fixtures for me, their faces and cries imprinted on my soul forever. In those moments, I realized why all the banter that happens around pregnancy feels so frivolous. The babies that I held were so real, solid, and important that they outweighed everything else. Each weighed just under 8 pounds, but the weight of their presence was infinite.

I wish that these moments had lasted, but as it happens, babies get hungry and cry, and the significance of the moment gets drowned out by lactation consultants and lack of sleep. I have regularly returned in my mind to these two moments to ask, what accounts for that moment of awe and power? Is it just hormones that bond me to my biological children, or is there something else?

I have also asked, simply, when I hold my children, what am I holding? Are they a beautiful accident of evolution that happened to get a bit of help from doctors and fertility treatments? Or does this moment indicate something deeper, a glimpse that there is something more to us than the miraculous combination of flesh, muscles, bones, and brains?

This question is not just about my children; it's about every child. It is about you, too, and every person you have ever known, those you have loved and hated. Are we just accidents? Or are we something more? Are we just physical creatures, or could we be spiritual too? At the core of the question about my children is the core of the question about the human experience: is all that we see all that there is?

Could we be more? Could we be infinite? Could we, by chance or providence, be eternal souls?

What Is A Soul?

The word soul is often misused, as if it is an organ like an appendix. We are glad that we have one but are rarely sure what it does. In Genesis 2:7, when God created a man, God formed the man from water and the dust of the earth. God brought this formation to life with breath/Spirit, and "the man became a living soul" (KJV). The man became a whole person. A soul is more than a tiny organ. It encompasses the wholeness of someone. It is mind. It is body. It is spirit. It is emotions. It is all of that wrapped up together.

We don't often describe our souls this way. In a 1907 experiment, popularized by Dan Brown's book, *The Lost Symbol,* a doctor named Duncan MacDougall hypothesized that the soul is distinct from the rest of the body. Testing the theory that each soul has a physical weight, as does every other organ, he measured the weight of six people as they died. Assuming the soul would depart from the body at the precise moment of death, the difference in weight would offer evidence of the presence of a soul. Dr. MacDougall concluded that a soul weighs ¾ of an ounce, or 21 grams.[1]

Called the "21 Grams Experiment," it is now an example of bad science but good entertainment. Only one of the patients in MacDougall's study lost 21 grams. The others either lost more or less, or they were entirely discounted as they died before the equipment was fully ready.[2] Books, songs, podcasts, television shows, and movies have leveraged this flawed but fascinating study. It has helped to shape a contemporary understanding of the soul as a tiny (¾ of an ounce) part of our bodies. With that image in our heads, we have misread Jesus. In the Gospel of Matthew, Jesus asks the rhetorical question: "What good will it be for someone to gain the whole world, yet forfeit their soul? Or what can anyone give in exchange for their soul" (Matthew 16:26)? If Jesus had MacDougall's experiment in mind, he would seem to be setting up a proposition where, in a spiritual black market, you can give up an apparently unusable 21 gram organ and receive whatever you wish.

This is the plot of the famous song by The Charlie Daniels Band, "The Devil Went Down to Georgia." In it, the devil discovers a young man named Johnny and offers a bet for the young man's soul. Johnny challenges the devil, saying, "I'll bet a fiddle of gold against your soul, 'cause I think I'm better than you."[3] With that, they proceed to play a competitive fiddle contest in which the stakes are Johnny's soul versus a fiddle of gold.

The idea of a soul as a possession to use is not unique. A sixteenth-century German legend tells the story of a man named Faust who makes a deal with a devilish figure named Mephistopheles. In the story, Faust exchanges his soul for a number of years of service.

Johnny's victory over the devil glosses over the reality of what losing a soul truly is: eternal enslavement. As the soul is the whole person, to lose one's soul is to lose one's self. In the Faust story, the devil does Faust's bidding for a time, but the tradeoff for a few years of power is an eternity of hell. Who would make such a trade? This is the point that Jesus was making: who would choose to give up their "self" to have more of something else? As I held my children, I discovered that they were more than the sum of their parts. If it is true of my children, it is true of every child of God. Even me.

The Toddler Dilemma

The fantastic and difficult thing about babies is that they grow up. As I write this in the middle of 2020, Sam is two and a half, and Ella Reece is eight months old. Life has changed from that first moment of cuddling. My days now contain hide and seek, hitting baseballs and golf balls, and trying to keep Sam from hugging his little sister with too much force. Before the COVID pandemic struck and the world seemingly shut down on March 12, 2020, we were busy. My life was filled with meetings and work; my wife stayed home with our baby, and Sam explored his first year of preschool. During the shutdown, I spent all my time with my wife and these two beautiful, young souls. I discovered the gift of going more slowly and watching my children more closely.

My personal experience revealed that parenting is less a grand strategy than the culmination of a million decisions. Here is a sampling of decisions (and decisions from those decisions) within a typical morning in our home:

- **When Sam wakes up, do we let him watch television while we make coffee and wake up?**
  - What show do we let him watch? Do we try for an educational show?
  - Is it okay for us to catch up on the news on our phone while he watches television? Or do we sit down with him and enjoy that time together?
  - If Sam is watching a show, do we try to limit the amount of television time that Ella Reece has since she is even younger? If so, what do we do with her in those moments?

- **What are we going to do for breakfast?**
  - Sam is asking for a granola bar. Do we give it to him to make him happy in that moment, or do we push for a real breakfast with better nutritional value?
  - Now that Ella Reece needs both a bottle and real food, how do we arrange doing all of that with Sam?
  - He wants to help with the baby. Do we let him try to feed his little sister when we know it will result in a mess?

These are just some of the questions that we face before 8:00 a.m.

During this particularly odd time of COVID quarantine that we are living through as I write this, I try to work while Becky facilitates the kids playing together. While Ella Reece is down for a nap, Becky works on teaching Sam some of what he would have learned in preschool before it shut down for the year. By the time the workday is done, we have time for a short walk and dinner—which has its own sets of questions and difficulties—before we put them down to bed. Then we attempt to clean the house before we go to bed and start again the next day.

This is a typical day for us. While your day may look different, everyone with children seems to be filled with endless queries about every imaginable thing. Parents's hours are filled with tasks, laundry, dishes, and a million questions about how we will survive each moment of that particular day. Yet, no matter how chaotic the day might get, we should be aware that our children are not problems for us to solve but fully human beings with their own unique thoughts and emotions. Every decision we make affects both them and us. Every day's choices shape not just today's mood or tomorrow's activities, but our eternal souls. Values and identities are shaped between meals and laundry. The truth of that first moment when we held those children close after they were born still feels just as true each and every day as they grow older. And we realize over and over again that our children were not an accident, not a task or burden, but a beautiful gift from God.

Every child is an eternal soul.

We can sometimes get so lost in our daily struggles that we miss the reality that this toddler throwing a fit today will grow up, will someday love and impact other humans, and will live on for eternity. That beautiful and intimidating truth gets swamped by the tiny and insignificant questions of day-to-day tasks. We can become so overwhelmed by the questions that pop up in daily life that we can lose sight of our role in shaping and guiding their souls. But we hope that, someday, we will live, not only this life with them, but that we will live with them in eternity.

How Do We See What We Really Are?

Like our children, we too are eternal. C. S. Lewis writes:

> There are no ordinary people. You have never talked to a mere mortal. Nations, cultures, arts, civilizations—these are mortal, and their life is to ours as the life of a gnat. But it is immortals whom we joke with, work with, marry, snub, and exploit—immortal horrors or everlasting splendors.[4]

As Paul writes in 1 Corinthians 15:53, "For this perishable body must put on the imperishable, and this mortal body must put on immortality" (ESV). Everyone who speaks of a soul does so with the belief that there is something beyond this life. The idea of a soul is compatible with many philosophies, religions, movies, and books. Plato, six orthodox schools of Hinduism, Jesus, and Pixar have all assumed that we have souls that are eternal. But what does that actually mean? What continues on after death? How can we see what we really are?

The Christian framework for the soul is simple and yet misunderstood. It is found in one brief line of the Apostle's Creed: "I believe in the resurrection of the body." This simple phrase is often overlooked, because the typical church member assumes that Christians are talking only about Jesus. The early followers of Jesus told of his death at the hands of the Romans, but they also talked about Jesus rising from the dead and eating and drinking with them before he ascended into heaven. This experience was so strong and explicit that they were willing to die rather than recant the story. Part of the reason they were willing to undergo death was their solid belief that what happened to Jesus will happen to us, that we too will have resurrected bodies. Paul writes, "Christ has indeed been raised from the dead, the firstfruits of those who have fallen asleep. . . . [I]n Christ all will be made alive" (1 Corinthians 15:20, 22). Christians from Paul to today have proclaimed that what continues after death is a new version of everything that we are. Our bodies, thoughts, emotions, and life will somehow be made whole.

What does that look like? No one knows. One church thinker from the fourth century, Gregory of Nyssa, imagined that every single part of us (including our hair) would be revived in resurrection. In seminary, my colleagues and I liked to joke that we would all have an end-times afro. In a more significant sense, it means that those who lose limbs or have cancer eat away at their bodies will have their bodies restored. The promise of eternity is that we will be made whole again. Death will not have the last say, and even the parts of us that we mourn and grieve will be made whole. This, of course, depends on whether we choose heaven. In Jesus's stories and metaphors, we learn that we are given that choice.

In his most famous teaching, the "Sermon on the Mount," Jesus tells the crowd watching him, "You are the salt of the earth." But he warns them that "if the salt loses its saltiness, how can it be made salty again? It is no longer good for anything, except to be thrown out and trampled underfoot" (Matthew 5:13). Harsh, yet true. The crowd (and we who are reading it) have the choice to be salt or something insignificant. God set up a world in which we get to choose to be salt—or not.

This demand for a choice is even more stark when Jesus gets specific:

You have heard that it was said, 'You shall not commit adultery.' But I tell you that anyone who looks at a woman lustfully has already committed adultery with her in his heart. If your right eye causes you to stumble, gouge it out and throw it away. It is better for you to lose one part of your body than for your whole body to be thrown into hell. And if your right hand causes you to stumble, cut it off and throw it away. It is better for you to lose one part of your body than for your whole body to go into hell (Matthew 5:27-30).

Jesus's example forced me to reimagine every single part of my life, not just the big decisions. Often, I would rationalize that some little choice I made wasn't that bad, but that is because I did not understand that every action I take has some small part in eternity. How could Jesus say that it is better for us to pluck out our right eye than to lust? It is because we cannot yet see what a lifetime of choosing lust (or anger, envy, or greed) does to our soul.

If we choose heaven, one day we will see with eternal eyes. While our bodies are bound to this world and the limitations of it, Jesus promises that our lives can be redeemed. Jesus describes heaven as an eternal home where there are many rooms, a banquet where we all get to feast, and a place of joy and love. Our entire person, including our body, will somehow be changed and redeemed, and we will sit with loved ones around the throne of God forever.

Or we won't. We will choose something else, and our souls will diminish and become less than what they could be. We are making choices right now that are either making our souls more solid or more shriveled and puny. Our souls are not something that we will have one day; they are our whole self, making eternal decisions at this very moment. We simply need new ways to recognize our choices.

As a pastor, one of the gifts that I have is the ability to be with people for a long time. I have been a pastor at the same church for ten years, and the founding pastor has been at this same church for thirty-four years. I have walked with families through ups and downs, divorces and marriages, children and miscarriages, death, job loss, and new careers. This unique lens has allowed me to see how the choices we make affect our souls and those around us.

One person that I met with as a pastor lost his marriage due to his decision to have an affair. He knew he had messed up, and it had deeply affected his life and his relationship with his grown children. After some time had passed after the divorce, this person asked me whether he could or should continue dating the person with whom he had the affair. Should he marry her?

For a moment, put yourself in my shoes. Here is a friend who is asking me a yes or no question. On what basis could I say yes or no? One of my core beliefs as a pastor is that I am called to help people see truth, but that God is the judge of all things. I have discovered that people often ask me for spiritual permission for something they have already decided to do, rather than asking what they ought to do. We need a better way to help people understand what is at stake in the questions they ask. So instead of giving him the answer, I asked him, "When you look at yourself five years from now, what do you want to see?"

He responded, "I want a good relationship with my children."

I described for him the concept of a solid soul, and a scenario in which his children look back five years from now and see someone who has made choice after choice to cultivate a good soul, one that prioritized the relationships in his life that he valued most. I asked him, "If you can imagine yourself at a holiday gathering in five years, knowing you have great relationships with your children, what choices did you make to get you there?"

Five years is often the time frame that I ask people to think about, because it is close enough to the present that we can begin to imagine our life then but far enough away that we can imagine living differently. We are bad at predicting what our lives will be like. A leadership maxim, variously attributed, states that people tend to overestimate what can be done in one year and underestimate what can be done in ten years. The same is true with our souls, except that our time frame is eternity. We often make decisions and then discover the consequences. Like Faust, we do not understand that our consequences are eternal.

Perhaps you want to know what my friend chose. The most important question is not what he chose but what would you choose? What choices are you making right now? Are they helping you become a solid soul? If you keep asking good questions and choosing the path that Jesus describes—choosing to cultivate a more solid soul—then heaven is before you, no matter what choices you have made in the past.

An Eternal Trajectory

The necessary lens that shapes our thinking about life requires us to remove the artificial division between life here on earth and life eternal. Jesus's message in all four Gospels is that the kingdom of heaven is here now. The choices that we make in every moment lead us toward heaven or away from it. We see this all around us in people who make choices and reap difficult consequences. People who choose their career over their families seem sad in the end, even if they have the trappings of wealth around them. People who choose grudges and anger over forgiveness and self-sacrifice later find themselves to be unhappy and isolated. These are the kinds of choices we make every single day—thousands of times every single day—and we often fool ourselves into thinking that our choices do not have an impact on our whole selves.

A solid soul is one that chooses to become the fullest version of what we could be. We choose to engage in our families, jobs, friendships, and lives in a way that beneficially impacts everyone around us, because that is what God did for us. Perhaps you know people in whom it is obvious that their decisions have formed them into beautiful souls, who make everyone and everything around them richer. Or perhaps you know people who have chosen the opposite. These people represent shriveled souls who tend to tear others down and create division and strife wherever they are. These are people who make bad choices over and over again.

Choosing wisely is not magic; it is about trajectory. We all make choices every day that lead us toward or away from a more solid life. As I parent, I make some good choices and some not-so-good choices. It isn't as though one bad choice can derail us, or one good choice can compensate for a lifetime of bad ones. Any attempt to put all people into a category of saints or sinners is doomed to fail. We are all complicated, eternal creations. But as souls, we can shape our trajectory by each day choosing heaven more often than hell. We can choose to seek a better way to live and a more positive way to impact those around us.

I will not be a perfect parent to Ella Reece and Sam. I will fail and sometimes make bad choices. But how I react to those choices will determine what happens next. When I get angry at my children and explode, do I double down on my anger and let them suffer in silence? Or do I choose a different path, apologize, hold them in my arms, and tell them I love them? These are not insignificant questions. These are eternal questions.

Soul Awareness

Out of all of the advice that I got when I had children, the one thing that cannot be overstated is how fast time flies. I have had many conversations with church members and friends about the fleeting nature of life. How we choose to spend our time here on earth determines whether we will make memories that we either cherish or regret. Good decisions matter. Quality time matters. It seems that the busier we get and the more we become consumed with everyday tasks and minuscule details, the faster time slips away. When we focus too much on the mortal and temporary, we can miss out on what truly matters.

For example, some people spend more time worrying about their school than their souls. This often plays out in rivalries. People from Texas A&M talk regularly about not wanting their children to wear the burnt orange of the University of Texas. Conversely, parents from the University of Texas don't want their children to wear the maroon of Texas A&M.

My family is from Kansas. I am a fourth generation Kansas Jayhawk. The Jayhawks of Lawrence, Kansas, have had a rivalry with the Missouri Tigers from Columbia, Missouri, since the 1860s. I could easily find quite a lot of energy for pushing my child away from Missouri. In days long ago, I have said that I would pay for any college for my child except for the University of Missouri. But does it really matter? The truth is, I would prefer that my children love God and neighbor as a Missouri Tiger than reject God and neighbor as a Kansas Jayhawk. I'm sure that is true for most people. But then, why do we put so much energy into decisions that make no difference to our souls and theirs?

Almost all questions posed to teenagers and college students are unrelated to their souls. What are you going to do when you graduate? Are you going to school? Which school? What will you major in? Will you join a sorority or a fraternity? There are people in every career and from every school who are moral and successful people, and people in every career and from every school who are immoral and unsuccessful people. Our children's careers and schools have nothing to do with their souls.

It does not matter *where* our children go to school; it matters eternally *who* they are at whatever school they attend or whatever job they take. It matters whether they are kind to those whom they encounter. It matters whether they make wise decisions that lead them to develop a solid soul or decisions that damage them for years to come. Like all of us, they will make eternal choices with every one of a thousand decisions every single day. My children are eternal souls. Helping them learn how to cultivate a solid soul is the most important thing I can do as a parent.

The purpose of this book is to help you see your life and the lives of others with eternal eyes. Each chapter in the book is intended to help you understand the immediate and eternal consequences of your daily choices, to increase your awareness and insight, to help you care more deeply and love more fully, and to make choices that reflect your values, your goals, and above all, your faith. As you read, I hope you will take the time to think in new ways about your relationships and the choices that define them. With God, it's never too late. You too can choose to have a solid soul.

PART ONE

It's All
About Soul

I have had the privilege of meeting several people whose souls are solid. They are simply different. You have their full attention when you are in their presence, and yet they do not pander to you. They are not seeking your affirmation but rather your friendship. They are kind, and yet you know they have a purpose and a clarity about their identity that drives their lives. There is nothing academic or hazy about a solid soul, and yet it seems very difficult to put into words or to imagine how we might pursue such a bold goal, especially when the world seems so at odds with the idea. Often, it is difficult to imagine how to have a solid soul when people who have them seem so rare. Could you become one of those rare people?

It is easier to imagine the opposite, having a shriveled soul. We know people like this. Likely, we are related to at least one of those people. In our more honest moments, we know people who would say this about us. The third chapter of this section will describe a "shriveled soul" in more detail. It is the shortest chapter of the entire book, because there isn't much to say about a shriveled soul. All shriveled souls are alike in that they choose themselves over everything else, and so the soul shrivels.

So how can you cultivate a solid soul? First, you need to know a little more about the nature of your soul. This section is intended to help you better understand what a soul is and how to describe it. Souls are best described within relationships. Marriage, for example, is a relationship between two souls. What is a marriage? A marriage is the gradual bonding and merging of two souls. Marriage grows over time by interactions forged between two souls. The choices they make toward each other and the rest of the world determine the bond that is formed. A marriage forms over time by intentional choices, thousands of tiny interactions, which result in a solid marriage, or not. This is true for each of us individually as well. Every day, we make decisions that become a part of our core identity. That core is eternal.

1 | Choose To Be Whole

It Never "Just Happens"

What would you do if you found yourself in an industry where it seemed everyone was cheating? This was the world of construction in the 1970s and early 1980s. Newspapers from this era tell stories about how the defrauding of the American public was uncovered. The *New York Times* says that evidence of fraud came to light due to a price discrepancy at a Virginia airport.[1] Other newspapers say it began at Chicago O'Hare airport when federal agents received complaints that people were rigging bids.[2] What is clear is that what began in one small sector—the building of airports—spread across highway bidding jobs in numerous states, including Illinois, Tennessee, Georgia, Virginia, Mississippi, Florida, Nebraska, Kansas, North Carolina, Kentucky, Louisiana, and Arkansas.[3] This was not a single instance of collusion but an entire industry defrauding the American public.

To explain this process, we must understand how bidding typically takes place on construction jobs. An agency of the United States or state government commissions designs for projects to be built and then sends out plans for bid. Companies then place bids on how much it may cost them to accomplish the plans. The lowest bid on the necessary specifications wins. This is true for construction, the military, and even NASA. As astronaut John Glenn stated, "As I hurtled through space, one thought kept crossing my mind—every part of this rocket was supplied by the lowest bidder."[4] Every American who drives on roads and across bridges could have that same feeling.

It gets worse in the story we are telling. Construction projects weren't granted to the lowest bidder because the bids were rigged.

Bid rigging is not complicated to conceive or accomplish. Say there are five companies, and they typically bid on a certain size and type of project, such as an asphalt road. All five are involved in various communities in a small state. The employees of these companies are members of churches and masonic lodges and have worked together legally for years. Often, one of the companies gets a big job, and they hire one of the other companies to assist them. They are used to being both competitors and partners. One year, perhaps one friend falls on hard times because some projects turned out to be more expensive than usual. The company is about to fail. What can that person's friends do about it? Simple. They can all bid high on the next project. It would be easy to justify: "Our friend has had a bad year. We don't need this project, and our friend does." Perhaps they reason, "The state of Kansas and the highway program are better if our friend doesn't go under. They need a little bit of help." Bid rigging is an agreement by those who can do the job *not* to bid competitively.

Over time however, one becomes two, and two becomes three, and the pattern of noncompetition becomes the way things are. This defrauds Americans, and yet it has happened across the industry in at least a dozen states.

What would you do? This was the question that faced William (Bill) H. Reece in 1980, as the second-generation owner and CEO of Reece Construction Company. He was also my grandfather.

What Happens When We Face An Ethics Question In Real Life?

The question of integrity and souls is not hypothetical or merely academic. It is worked out in the everyday questions of real life. Most of the owners were not in the construction industry to defraud the American public. Their goal was to build America. Many, like my grandfather, served in World War II at great cost and sacrifice. It is important to highlight that these were not people who began with malevolent intentions. And yet, in the early 1980s, they found themselves in a federal courtroom faced with prison sentences and fines, both corporate and personal.[5]

What happened?

I was not able to interview any of the men who went to prison or paid fines in the scandal, but to a large extent the pattern is consistent in most every conversation that I have had in ministry in which people describe how they got to where they are. Wives who have had an affair say, "I never set out to cheat on my husband; it just happened." People who end up stealing large amounts often begin with a small amount for what is, in their mind, a justified reason. Some people in this world do set out to lie, cheat, and steal, but that isn't most people. Most people seem to claim, at least, that it "just happens."

How could that be? How could stealing money or defrauding the American public just happen? The difficulty is that almost all big decisions start small. Often, we do not know that we are even making them. We like to think that the questions that define us are clear and unambiguous, like the choice of going to college. While I wanted to attend only one college and applied to only one college, I am in the vast minority. My friends applied to multiple colleges, weighed scholarships and majors, and made a deliberate choice. This is how ethics is often taught.

The television show, *The Good Place*, is about an ethical afterlife where people either go to a "good place" or a "bad place" based on how ethically they lived their lives. In one of the episodes, the writers dramatize a stereotypical, academic, ethical question named "The Trolley Problem." This problem has an infinite number of variables, but it is framed like this:

There is a runaway trolley barreling down the railway tracks. Ahead, on the tracks, there are five people tied up and unable to move. The trolley is headed straight for them. You are standing some distance off in the train yard, next to a lever. If you pull this lever, the trolley will switch to a different set of tracks. However, you notice that there is a person on the side-track. You have two options:

1) **Do nothing and allow the trolley to kill the five people on the main track.**

2) **Pull the lever, diverting the trolley onto the side-track where it will kill one person.**

Which is the more ethical option? Or, more simply: What is the right thing to do?[6]

While the "Trolley Problem" makes for excellent television, it is so hypothetical as to be virtually pointless. The real danger is when we believe that ethics decisions are this dramatic and clear. In the "Trolley Problem," the choice is clear: do nothing or pull the lever. The consequence is clear: five lives lost or one life lost. But this clarity is false. Who put the people on the tracks? Why are you in this position to decide? Are you sure that these are the only options? And more important, what happens to your soul in either choice?

A version of this question is found in the Batman movie *The Dark Knight,* in which the Joker reveals two boats, one with convicted criminals and the other with civilians. Each group has the ability to blow up the other. They will both blow up if neither boat chooses to blow up the other one. What do you do? Spoiler alert: My favorite part of the movie is the surprise that neither the criminals nor the civilians chose to detonate the other boat. The civilians voted to blow up the boat with the criminals, but no one would personally push the button. In the boat with the criminals, an evidently hardened criminal takes the detonator and throws it out the window, so as not to tempt anyone else.[7]

I believe *The Dark Knight*'s premise to be true: when faced with clear and immediate consequences, we rarely do the bad thing. But that is not life. Life, marriage, and work are messy and complicated. Often, we do not understand the consequences of our decisions for a very long time, and we sometimes choose poorly.

It Is A Small World

The highway construction industry is a small world, especially in a state like Kansas. Reece Construction Company was founded in 1926 by my great-grandfather. My grandfather took over for his father after World War II, and my mother took over for him in the 1980s. My sister is in the process of becoming the fourth-generation owner/president. Members of my family have been doing this for almost 100 years, which means that the people who were involved in the scandal that opened this chapter were not evil, nameless people. They were friends and competitors. They worked together in an organization called AGC (Association of General Contractors) in the state of Kansas to make the state and the industry better. In their small world, where everyone seemed to know everyone, there was a culture and community of helping each other out. The community set up an environment that enabled collusion.

There are two basic facts about bid rigging:

1) **It is very easy to do.**
2) **It takes just one person to stop it.**

Stopping illegal collusion is technically simple but emotionally problematic. If one owner refuses to play the game, then bid rigging cannot happen. In this type of system, peer pressure to conform to the way things are done is massive. Consistently bidding at the proper price can end the entire collusion.

So, what do you do? Do you let your friend go under? Do you tell your other friends no, even when it appears unlikely you will be caught and everyone else is doing it? What if you say no? What if it were you who needed the job to keep your family afloat and your employees working? Any consequences would be difficult to prove and a long way away. What if you did it just this once?

What Is Wrong With Just A Little Wrong?

Every day of our lives, we are faced with choices in which we know that there is a right thing to do, but we just don't want to do it. We know that we ought to quit smoking, eat vegetables, get more than eight hours of sleep every night, go to church every week, exercise more, drink less alcohol, and eat less ice cream. As the television show *Sweet Magnolias* says, "Doctors and preachers tell you to give up stuff you already know isn't good for you."[8] It seems impossible to do everything right, so what is the harm in a little wrong?

The answer lies in the trajectory. Nothing is ever static. We humans are creatures of habit. A single behavior results in another behavior, and those behaviors compound. Ice cream as an occasional treat is no problem. Ice cream as a habit is a major problem. Alcohol in moderation is not a problem, until it is impossible to do in moderation. A night out with the friends rather than at home with your spouse is a great thing done occasionally. Do it more and more regularly, and your marriage will suffer. Golf is a great activity and sport, but we have a name for a situation in which a couple is married but her husband is always out playing golf. We call the wife a "golf widow." I have been warned not to turn my wife into a golf widow.

This is not to say that a little collusion or cheating is fine. We spend a lot of our lives feeling like we are making compromises—in our diets, in our marriages, with our children, and in our lives—and it leads to the question: "What is one more?" Such compromises can lead us to a place where we erode who we wish to be. Ten or twenty years later, we wake up in poorer physical shape than we want to be, in relationships with our children that are not the best, in marriages that are shells of their former selves, and in jobs in which we have compromised our potential and our integrity.

No one cheats on his or her spouse because of one decision. It may feel like it just happened, but it was the result of 150 decisions, not just one. It was the decision to emotionally confide in someone to whom you were attracted. The decision not to wear a wedding ring on a business trip. The decision to stay at the bar later than is wise. The decision to scoot the chair just a little closer to another person. The decision to touch another person with just a graze to see how he or she might respond. By the time an actual decision to have sex happens, it feels like "it just happened," but that was the trajectory you were already on.

What is wrong with a little wrong? Little wrongs can too easily lead to big wrongs.

Another trajectory is one in which we make intentional and deliberate choices about who we wish to be, keeping an eye on the trajectory of our lives. A few years ago, my church sent our COO and me through a year-long management training course, in which the session leader probed deeply into the core values and purpose of our lives. This was a life changing and eye-opening year for me. It forced me to engage in my values and to develop a process for evaluating the choices I was making. Fundamentally, the leaders of the course were trying to adjust our lives to be more congruent with our values.

I discovered in this process how hard it is to name values and keep them. One place of conversation in the process was on the question of exercise. In my first draft of values, I said that I cared deeply about exercise. Both my friend and my coach said that they did not believe me. If I cared about exercise, I would exercise more. At the time, I was about twenty-five pounds larger than I should have been, and while I occasionally exercised, it had never been a priority in my life. Instead, I realized that my true value was my ability to go on adventurous trips with my family. One of my favorite trips growing up was a week-long canoeing trip through the border waters of the United States and Canada. I became aware that my value was not exercising, per se, but being fit enough to be able to do those types of trips with my wife and children.

Since then, I have exercised more, lost those twenty-five pounds, and am happier with my body. On those days or weeks when I do not exercise, I do not believe that I am compromising my values, because I am still on a trajectory that will allow me to go on hikes with my children when I am 65 years old. I enjoy ice cream with my family because my family, not my body, is my primary value after my faith.

Naming values helps us avoid compromising them. When we are clear about who we want to be and are congruent with it, we can imagine the trajectory of who we wish to become. A single decision is not just one decision. It is part of a larger trajectory of who we are becoming. This is not about being perfect. It is not about never making mistakes. It is understanding that the choices we make now have a ripple effect for the rest of our lives, and often, we do not even know that we are making them.

Bad Choices Ripple Out

One reason that we choose to compromise at work when we would not in other parts of our lives is that we imagine that parts of our lives are segmented from others. Too many people have told me that they have their Christian lives, and then they put on their game face and go to their day jobs. They tell me it seems almost impossible to navigate work life with the same faith and commitments they have to family. Work is work, they suggest, and family is family. With this thinking, we are shape shifters who become whoever we need to be in whatever context we find ourselves in. Or at least we think we do.

Compartmentalization is a figment of our imagination. Who you are at work or school impacts how you interact with your spouse or children at home. The friends that teenagers hang out with at school impact who they are at home. The same is true for their parents. Every single part of life is connected because each part of our lives impacts our souls. This book contains numerous chapters focusing on different sections of life: integrity, marriage, children, and work. But a solid soul is someone who is whole, unsegmented, and uncompartmentalized. Our lives are not snapshots of an ethics or business class with a question about a trolley in a hypothetical world. We are souls who engage in work, play, and love, and it is impossible to segment one part of our souls from another without doing damage to their integrity.

One of the people sentenced in the bid-rigging scheme was a friend of my grandfather. He was a minor figure in the scheme, judged by the dollar amounts and jail sentence levied by the US District Court Judge. He had this to say in the courtroom: "I apologize and am sorry for what has happened and what we have done. It will never happen again."[9] The newspaper writer covering the case noted that this was said as the man's wife and daughter wept in the courtroom. This man's initial decision to participate in the widespread scheme was far removed from the consequences of admitting guilt in court while his wife and daughter wept. Like the characters on the boat in The Dark Knight, he would never have pushed that button if he could have seen the future consequences of jail and a weeping family. Segmenting our moral choices from the rest of our lives is a lie; the choice to cut a corner is never just about one person. It is about a community of people, including the people whom we love the most in the world. When we are confronted with a tiny choice, the resulting ripple effect impacts, not just us and the rest of our lives, but the rest of the lives of everyone whom we love. In my research, I found the obituary of the man in this story. It mentions nothing about bid rigging and jail. What he told the judge proved to be true. He changed. He paid his debt for his choice and chose a different path where he would become a leader in a better industry.

Reclaiming The Soul

Part of the goal of this book is to reclaim the word soul. When we redefine the word soul in terms of our whole self, we can see how our choices have a significant impact on who we are and what that means for our future. If choices impact our souls, and our souls are eternal, then we must develop a much longer view of who we wish to be. It is my hope that we can change the question of difficult choices from, "What should I do?" to "Which choice is best for my soul? Which choice makes me more whole?"

If we have a soul, then our souls can be redeemed. Ignoring that we have souls may have contributed to a world that assumes that one bad thought, word, or deed means you should be "canceled." As Christians, we don't believe a soul should be canceled; it should be redeemed. I believe my grandfather's friend was redeemed. That means that we have the chance of having even our worst choices made whole.

Jesus believed that we are worth redeeming. Not everyone who reads this book will believe in Jesus, and if this is you, I hope you still find value in the arguments and stories in this book. But I also ask you to indulge me for just a moment, as I tell you tell you why

Jesus matters. The basic message of Jesus when he walked the earth was simple: "The kingdom of God has come near. Repent and believe the good news" (Mark 1:15)! If I were to paraphrase Jesus, he would be saying, God has found a way to make the world right again! You are close to living the life that our Creator intended, but you have made some bad choices. Change your mind! Change your heart! Turn your life around! Believe the good news that God's redemption is possible for you!

I know this message to be true because Jesus had a choice to run away from his sacrifice on the cross but chose instead to be executed. He chose to go to the depths of pain and hell, so that you would not have to be alone. He rose from the grave, so that you could know that healing—even from death—is possible. We are eternal. God has given us a choice to live a full life by following Jesus and choosing heaven over hell. The concept of the eternal nature of our souls helps us understand what Jesus died for and what he redeemed.

Living For This Handshake

The bid-rigging story has been a legend in my family, not because it was sensational, but because of my grandfather. One day, in the small town of Scandia, Kansas, my grandfather heard a knock on the door. A man identified himself as a federal officer and then reached out for a handshake. He said, "Bill, I have spent two years investigating collusion and bid rigging. I have focused on Kansas. There is one area where we haven't seen any evidence of it. I was told that it was because there were two honest contractors in the state, and you are one of them. So, I drove all this way, because I simply wanted to shake your hand. Thank you."

I have heard this story my whole life. The older I get, the more I appreciate it. When I was younger, it was told as a statement of respect and appreciation for my grandfather. As I grew older and became a teenager, it was a helpful reminder of who I was expected to become. As an adult with children, I have come to be grateful for the example of this legacy. My grandfather did not simply pass down a company to his daughter and granddaughter but also a legacy of doing things the right way.

In talking to my mother about my grandfather's legacy, she challenged me to think more about the story of my grandfather's friends. They were people who made poor choices forty years ago and then chose to turn their lives around. They, too, have left a great legacy, one of repentance and the possibility to choose a different trajectory. Our souls are impacted by our choices, but they are not limited to them. Our choices can be redeemed by choosing at this moment to be who we wish to be. Our future souls are dependent upon us living a more integrated and congruent life, starting now.

2 | Heaven (Or Hell) Begins Now

Every year on the University of Kansas campus at Wescoe Beach, a man screamed at college girls, telling them they were going to hell when they died. To set the scene, you need to know a few things. First, Wescoe Beach is not a beach but rather a concrete slab in the middle of campus in front of an architectural tragedy, a bunker-like concrete building called Wescoe Hall. In an otherwise beautiful campus, Wescoe Hall is an ugly center point where most people congregate. All types of people hang out there: famous basketball players, sorority girls, student groups advertising to their community, and anyone who wants attention. Second, this man came here every year like clockwork to shout his epitaphs at the female students. In talking with other students at Big-12 schools somewhere around the same time, they all remembered a similar man with a similar message: "When you die, you are going to hell!" Third, the screaming man did not know any of the girls he was addressing. He just assumed that every girl was a sorority girl, and every sorority girl was on the harlot highway to hell. Needless to say, the guy was not very popular.

Inevitably, one person or another, usually a man, would decide to debate him, and satisfied that he had finally gotten a nibble on the end of his hook, he would berate the man, telling him that he was going to hell when he died. Christians often debated him, embarrassed at his example of Christianity. Other times, atheists debated with him the entire concept of God. Most times, people just shook their heads and walked on.

This happened every year. I never engaged with the man, but I had numerous problems with his approach. For one thing, I do not believe that any of us can judge someone else's soul. For another, he condemned everyone and did not show an ounce of compassion or grace. Out of all the debates with him that I overheard, I noted one premise of his that was never contested by anyone: hell or heaven exist but only after death.

A concert I went to in high school turned out to be an evangelism event. The pitch there was far more effective than that of the odd stranger on Wescoe Beach. Yet there too, the message focused on heaven and hell as a reality that happens only once we die. We even begin our jokes about hell or heaven with: "One day, so and so died, and he went to hell/heaven . . ." We are so accustomed to the assertion about hell or heaven existing after we die that we never truly stop to think about whether that is where it begins. When Jesus began teaching, his first message was "the kingdom of heaven has come near." Paul wrote in Romans, "I am convinced that neither death nor life, neither angels nor demons, neither the present nor the future, nor any powers, neither height nor depth, nor anything else in all creation, will be able to separate us from the love of God that is in Christ Jesus our Lord" (Romans 8:38-39). He was specifying that God's love and power exist before and after death. Heaven, in other words, is available now. Unfortunately, as long as brokenness and pain are so prevalent in our lives, it may be easier to believe that only hell is available now. But it is also possible to discover a better way.

Tangible Eternity

The greatest struggle in imagining heaven and hell on earth is that we are riddled with mental images of heaven and hell in the afterlife. Google searches of heaven consistently show clouds in a blue-sky background with a sunburst streaming out from behind the clouds. Sometimes there is a stairway to the clouds. Often the stairway is itself made of clouds. Take a second and imagine heaven. It probably looks a lot like this in your mind. Hell is an equally consistent image for us of flailing and screaming bodies in a pit or a lake of fire. If you take a moment and imagine a picture of hell, you will probably come up with a similar image.

But heaven and hell are not that simple, not even in scripture. One story of heaven and hell by Jesus in the Gospel of Matthew reveals a Roman centurion who comes and asks for help. For most Jews in Jesus's day, a centurion was an enemy, an oppressive military soldier, trained to hold down revolts and insurrections. On this day, though, the centurion came asking for help to heal his servant. Jesus asked him whether he should come and heal the man. The centurion replied that Jesus's physical presence would be unnecessary, saying, "Lord, I do not deserve to have you come under my roof. But just say the word, and my servant will be healed. For I myself am a man under authority, with soldiers under me. I tell this one, 'Go,' and he goes" (Matthew 8:8-9). Jesus replied by talking about heaven:

> Truly I tell you, I have not found anyone in Israel with such great faith. I say to you that many will come from the east and the west, and will take their places at the feast with Abraham, Isaac, and Jacob in the kingdom of heaven. But the subjects of the kingdom will be thrown outside, into the darkness, where there will be weeping and gnashing of teeth (Matthew 8:10-12).

In scripture, heaven is depicted, not as white clouds packed with uptight people, but rather as a wedding feast with Roman centurions sitting next to Abraham. I have often said that heaven is a feast where you are guaranteed to be surprised at who is sitting next to you. I have been to only a few parties like that here on earth where perfect food is matched with perfect company, but if that is what heaven is like, sign me up!

Hell, on the other hand, is isolation and pain, darkness and tears. The word hell was a recognizable topic to Jesus's listeners, as the word hell meant *Gehenna or the Valley of Hinnom*. This valley (hell) in the Scriptures was a "ravine south of Jerusalem where fires were kept burning to consume the dead bodies of animals, criminals, and trash."[1] It was a place of destruction and brokenness. Neither the concept of heaven as a feast nor hell as a fiery trash heap are like the intangible metaphors of a Google search, but rather the conclusions of our choices. To our modern ears, heaven could be described as a massive feast with Jesus, catered by the best Paris chef; and hell described as a local dump so vile that it often caught on fire.

As I have reflected about "preachers" on college campuses and the evangelism event I attended in high school, I have concluded that both undersold heaven and hell. Heaven and hell are not some distant events, but a choice in each moment. If heaven is a banquet, all the yelling about hell kept the preacher at Wescoe Beach from experiencing heaven that day. Wescoe Hall had a newly renovated food court that had just been completed. Perhaps a shared meal with those that he was condemning could have been a small taste of what heaven might look like. If heaven and hell can exist in the here and now, in what moments have we made decisions in favor of isolation and hell rather than embracing the opportunity of heaven?

Your Brain Is Lying To You

Dr. Laurie Santos, Professor of Psychology and Cognitive Science at Yale University, says that when we make bad choices, our brain is lying to us. Professor Santos created one of the most popular courses in the history of Yale, entitled "Psychology and the Good Life." She later made her class available online with a podcast called *The*

Happiness Lab. It is my personal favorite podcast because it provides brilliant insights and practical guidance. In the second episode of her podcast, "The Unhappy Millionaire," Dr. Santos says this:

> Research shows that we suck at predicting what will make us happy, generally, both when we are imagining what we will feel when we get what we want, the good stuff like hitting the jackpot, getting the perfect job, getting accepted to our dream school, but also when we experience some of the worst events that people could possibly endure. Why are we so bad at making these predictions? What's going wrong?
>
> Our minds are constantly telling us what to do to be happy. But what if our minds are wrong? What if our minds are lying to us, leading us away from what would really make us happy?[2]

In the episode, Dr. Santos shows examples of people winning the lottery and remaining unhappy, as opposed to people who have been in tragic accidents, who are happy and grateful for their past. Which would you prefer? To win the lottery? Or to be permanently injured in a massive accident? This isn't really a question. No one would ever pick a permanent injury over having massive amounts of money. And yet, if you looked a few years down the road, you might see that the person who won the lottery was miserable and ended his life with suicide, while the person who was tragically burned in the military was happy and thriving. Why?

If this is true, then how can we know what makes us happy?

Dr. Santos introduces strategies and frameworks to show how science has helped us uncover how to find true happiness, for example:

· **We need to talk to people.** Brief interactions such as in a checkout line or at the bank make people feel happy.

- *We need to minimize our choices.* We think we want a lot of choices in our lives, but too many choices can diminish our happiness. Dr. Santos also emphasizes gratitude, reframing our work and decisions, and removing distractions.

Though her purpose is to demonstrate what science can teach us about happiness, in *The Happiness Lab,* Dr. Santos is mostly articulating Christian beliefs. The phrase "our minds are lying to us, leading us away from what would really make us happy" is a perfect Christian definition of human sin and brokenness. I pay close attention to Dr. Santos's podcast, because it provides numerous strategies for understanding our brains and guides us in how to manipulate our minds to make better decisions for long-term happiness. The podcast is full of great illustrations for sermons and life, but it never answers the larger question about who we are. Aren't we our minds? Isn't our mind part of us? If our mind is lying to us, who is us?

Infinite Happiness

The difficulty with secular and scientific conversations around happiness is that there is an inevitable time limit to the conversation. If we humans were made for temporary happiness, then happiness is an actuarial question, the study of how long we likely will live on this earth. I am thirty six as I am writing this, and my expected lifespan, according to the Social Security Administration, is another 42.19 years.[3] I have a .22 percent chance of dying this year. If we are simply physical beings with one short life, how can we live out our lives in such a way that we maximize happiness?

As a teenager, I tried to intellectually work out the best strategy for having the most fun and still getting to heaven. Since I believed that Jesus would remove my sin if I prayed and asked forgiveness, it occurred to me that, if I knew when I was going to die, the best strategy would be for me to do whatever I wanted (alcohol, sex, drugs) and then ask for forgiveness later. The obstacle in my teenage brain (which was certainly lying to me regularly) was not knowing when I was going to die. So, I came up with a different strategy: I could keep sinning and simply ask for forgiveness regularly. My plan was to ask for forgiveness every week at church and then ignore faith from Monday through Saturday. If you were to ask my friends, they would tell you, I didn't do any of those things (sex, drugs, or alcohol) in high school, and there were two reasons. First, I was too intellectually honest to ask for forgiveness when I didn't mean it. But second, I realized that this was the wrong lens, because my friends who did those things weren't any happier.

An eternal lens changes the conversation because eternity begins now. In Lewis's book, *The Great Divorce*, one creature asks a spirit already in heaven, "What are we born for?" The spirit replies, "For infinite happiness . . . You can step into it at any moment."[4] Death, then, becomes a significant, but ultimately arbitrary moment in an eternal quest for joy and happiness. We can choose that eternal journey to infinite happiness right now.

Choose Heaven, Not Hell

The famous song, "James," by the band Blue October, has a frenzied intensity that matches its dark message. The song's second verse says:

> You're
> Not so brave,
> When I'm the snake
> And you're my prey.[5]

This song was published in 2004 on the live album *Argue with a Tree*. The introduction to the song by lead singer Justin Furstenfeld went like this: "There's some issues in life that you just gotta let go of, and there's one that I have never been able to. So tonight after this song, I'm letting this $#%@ go. This is a song about anger. This is a song about revenge."[6]

To me, this song, catchy as it is, sounds like living in hell. I lived in hell once. In chapter four, you will read more about my divorce from my college sweetheart. I once lived in a marriage that was crumbling. I felt isolated and lonely, seething at the consequences of my and my wife's choices. I felt anger and betrayal. The song by Blue October is popular because every person I know has some name that we can substitute in for "James." We all have the choice to live in hell. Everyone I have counseled as a pastor since my own divorce has confirmed that their divorce was like hell on earth. Every alcoholic or drug addict has told me that they have been through hell. But the good news about engaging with people who have been through hell is that it is not always an eternal destination. Going through hell implies that you can get to the other side.

On January 5, 2021, Blue October's Instagram posted a picture of Justin taking a selfie with another guy. The caption read:

> Over 20 years ago I wrote a song called James. The song was a dark piece about hateful revenge and jealousy. I still look back and dread the content sometimes. I always wrote from my heart and put everything into my songs, but this one was borderline threatening. I guess I wrote it to get through what happened between James and me and for a kind of self-therapy. But the fact of the matter is, the song was hateful and wicked.
>
> Fast forward to about two months ago. I was hiking, and I heard someone call my name. I turned around and

it was James. All I can say is that I instantly apologized for my behavior, and he did too. We also spoke of how finding a higher power and getting sober helped us both find peace and happiness. It was amazing and comforting to know that forgiveness is real. I believe that people can really change and grow over time. People are compassionate and caring at heart, and I'm so proud of both of us James. Thank you for stopping me, because I am a better person now because of this encounter.[7]

If we can go through hell while we are still alive and find heaven, as in this moment with Justin and James, maybe we can choose heaven now as well. We might get down on ourselves for not having chosen heaven earlier, but we could forgive ourselves and choose today to find a different path.

Our soul choices begin again every day. We can step into infinite joy at this very moment. We do not have to wait for tomorrow, the day after, or until after death to choose heaven. We can choose joy today.

3 | Shriveled Souls

Up to this point, I have focused on some positive stories of those who have chosen a path for becoming a solid soul. In chapter one, we looked at two such paths. One path revealed a man who chose not to engage in a scandal. The other path revealed a man, who after getting caught, turned his life around. Single, individual choices do not dictate where your soul will end up. Continually choosing well makes all the difference. Look at the story of Justin in chapter two, who found his way to recovery and reconciliation with James. They chose paths every day to become more solid.

To understand the value of a solid soul, we need to talk about what happens when we continually refuse to take the right path. Some never choose the right path. Even when heaven and joy are offered, some choose hell. Like a child that throws a tantrum while friends are over to play, each of us has the capacity to choose selfish isolation over joy and community. I occasionally did this when I was young. I would throw a fit and go sit in my room, hoping that someone would come and join me in my sulking. Eventually, I was given a choice: nurse my grievance or choose something better. In ten years of ministry, I have come face to face with the reality that people often choose a shriveled soul. The difficult truth is that every one of us makes these choices in some part of our life. We may nurse hurts or angers that would feel amazing to give up, but they have come too close to defining our identity for us to let go of them. Our grumblings have become part of our souls. To choose joy feels like we would lose part of ourselves.

What does that look like? What is a shriveled soul? Part two of the book will talk about how we navigate our soul in relationships: in our marriages and with our children, friends, and co-workers. Part three will talk practically about how we can set our souls on a new trajectory and together do and be more than we ever thought we could do and be. But to fully grasp the stakes, we need to be unambiguous about what happens to our souls when we choose poorly.

Destruction And Brokenness Look The Same

The rubble at the bottom of the twin towers on 9/11 was an image that was cemented into me as I, along with the rest of the world, grappled with the destruction of what had been strong and beautiful just moments before. Since that day, we have seen countless images of toppled buildings from wars in the Middle East or accidental bombings, such as the ammonium nitrate explosions of West, Texas in 2013, or Beirut in August 2020. Each time, the rubble looks the same.

Pristine cities like Paris and New York have their own style and unique beauty, but when destroyed, they all have the same dusty and pasty gray look to them. The same is true for our lives. When flourishing, for example, our marriages all have different tones and textures. There are a million ways to be happily married, but divorce always consists of separation and division, the ripple effects of mutual destruction. Flourishing businesses find countless ways to live out the goals and hopes of their organizations, but businesses that are dying all seem to have the same infighting and blaming. At the core of each bit of destruction is a sense of selfish isolation.

Consider a character we all know and love to hate: the Grinch. Dr. Seuss writes:

See every Who down in Whoville liked Christmas a lot . . . but the Grinch, who lived just north of Whoville, didn't! The Grinch hated Christmas! The whole Christmas season! Now, please don't ask why. No one quite knows the reason. And though it could've been that his head wasn't screwed on just right, or that his shoes were too tight, we find out that the most likely reason of all is that his heart was two sizes too small.[1]

The image of Whoville could represent a million different types of places or people. Communities have a habit of creating their own unique culture, but the image of the Grinch could have taken only one form: a grumbling, selfish, envious, pathetic, isolated person. The heart condition described by Dr. Seuss was not a medical condition but a metaphor for his soul. Of course, Dr. Seuss wrote that such a condition was reversible. On the day the Grinch chose a different path, his heart grew three sizes.

The Grinch is a universal image of a soul that has chosen poorly, that has focused inward on itself. One of C. S. Lewis's most quoted metaphors for this kind of soul comes from his essay, "The Weight of Glory." Lewis writes, "We are halfhearted creatures, fooling about with drink and sex and ambition when infinite joy is offered us, like an ignorant child who wants to go on making mud pies in a slum because he cannot imagine what is meant by the offer of a holiday at the sea. We are far too easily pleased."[2] Lewis's point is not that drink, ambition, and sex are bad things. The problem is that these things can destroy us if they become what we most desire. How many good men and women have chosen alcohol over their children, resulting in neglect or abuse? This is choosing hell on earth. How many have chosen ambition or sex and have left their values behind? Too many pastors and friends of mine have chosen ambition or sex and have ruined their ministries and often their marriages.

The results are always the same: devastation, isolation, and brokenness. But just as rubble can be cleared so that new cities emerge, our lives can turn around and find redemption. But often, violence and destruction simply become our way of life. As Alexander Hamilton says in the musical *Hamilton,* while worrying about the effects of the American revolution:

> Or will the blood we shed begin an endless
> Cycle of vengeance and death with no defendants?[3]

As we have seen in revolutions from the French Revolution in 1789 to the Arab Spring in 2010, vicious cycles often keep getting more vicious, and the rubble may not be cleared for generations. It just keeps piling on. Souls in these vicious cycles often choose not to grow three sizes in one day, but rather to keep shrinking.

Why Would Anyone Choose A Shriveled Soul?

A few years ago, I was introduced to a fascinating book called *The Power of TED*: The Empowerment Dynamic.* Written by David Emerald, the book is a modern fable that describes the difference between two types of human interaction: the "dreaded drama triangle" and "the empowerment dynamic." One is a vicious cycle that spirals downward, taking down all involved with it; the other is a virtuous cycle that exponentially improves life for all members in the relationship. The "dreaded drama triangle"(DDT) is a disempowering and vicious cycle that, while simplistic, is a familiar story. Within the triangle are three characters: a persecutor, a victim of that persecutor, and a rescuer of the victim.[4] DDT is like a game of rock/paper/scissors where everyone loses. It begins a vicious cycle with no way out. If the rescuer decides that the persecutor is now the enemy, the rescuer ends up becoming the persecutor, the persecutor ends up the victim, and the former victim now fills a new role as rescuer. In this way, relationships continue to perpetuate drama.

Let's say you are at a family dinner that has just finished. Dad (persecutor) says to Mom (victim), "Well, aren't you going to clean up?" Mom apologizes and rushes to the kitchen to do so. The child (rescuer) goes to the mom, puts one arm around her, and says "I'm so sorry that he is so rude to you. He is such a problem. Let me help you." The child says to Dad, "Why do you always do this? Who made you king?" With this, the roles are changing. Now the child (persecutor) yells at Dad (now the victim), and Mom (filling the role as rescuer) comes back to the table and says, "Oh, it's okay; I don't mind it." Drama.

According to the "Power of TED" website, "These drama roles are made-up strategies that [our] egos create to manage [our] anxiety about what [we don't] like or want."[5] These drama triangle roles were originally revealed by Dr. Stephen Karpman, a professor of psychology, in the 1960s, and have been used to describe a vicious cycle of disempowerment and drama in family and work systems.

Each of these types of personalities and their interlocking relationships have a system that, although dysfunctional and disempowering, has worked for the players up until that point. If complaining gets you a new meal at a restaurant, maybe you keep complaining. If grumbling gets you attention, maybe you keep grumbling. You will see people keep choosing a shriveled soul, because it feels easier to choose something lesser than to forge a different path or form a new trajectory. Consider this vignette from the tenth chapter of Lewis's *The Great Divorce*. The speaker is a wife from hell asking to have her husband (who has chosen a different path to heaven) sent back to hell with her:

> You haven't the faintest conception of what I went through with your dear Robert. The ingratitude! It was I who made a man of him! Sacrificed my whole life to him! And what was my reward? Absolute, utter selfishness. No, but listen. He was pottering along on about six hundred a year when I married him. And mark my words, Hilda, he'd have been

in that position to the day of his death if it hadn't been for me. It was I who had to drive him every step of the way. He hadn't a spark of ambition. It was like trying to lift a sack of coal. I had to positively nag him to take on that extra work in the other department. . . . Please please! I'm so miserable. I must have someone to—to do things to. It is simply frightful down there. No one minds about me at all.[6]

This is the truth about shriveled souls and selfish isolation. We want others in hell with us. "Misery loves company" is the way we usually hear it. Misery craves company and will create drama to get it. Shriveled souls do not want simply to remain shriveled and leave everyone else alone but to tear others down with them. Nothing makes shriveled souls feel punier than to be around those whose souls are solid. The goal of the shriveled soul then is to bring their solid soul compatriots down to their level. Why would anyone choose a shriveled soul? People do it every day because it seems to work for them in the present, even if in the end it results in hell. In the introduction, we highlighted that losing a soul is eternal enslavement. The enslavement is of our own choosing! If we choose selfishness for long enough it becomes the pattern that determines our lives and we become enslaved to our selfishness. If our anger consumes us, we become defined by our anger and it binds us.

An eternity of blame, selfishness, and drama can consume us, so that we are almost indistinguishable from our complaints. A shriveled soul is not about a single choice. There are murderers and thieves in heaven right now. There are people on death row—as Jesus was once upon a time—with solid souls. Shriveled souls are those who have chosen a path of selfish isolation for so long and so many times that they are a tiny fraction of their former selves.

Shriveled, But Not Hopeless

Saint Augustine wrote that the state of the soul is so bent and broken that it can only stare at itself.[7] The soul that has chosen a shriveled existence with a myriad of complaints and grievances is the trajectory of the Grinch, but sadly, it is more common than the trajectory of hope. I have known more people who have chosen anger, greed, envy, and lust than have rejected it. Jesus instructed his listeners, "Enter through the narrow gate. For wide is the gate and broad is the road that leads to destruction, and many enter through it. But small is the gate and narrow the road that leads to life, and only a few find it" (Matthew 7:13-14).

The easy path is to the shriveled soul. Compared to a solid soul, a shriveled one is flimsy and insignificant. Hell is described as a "weeping and gnashing of teeth," and people imagine that it is because God is punishing them by a demon with a pitchfork for choices from which they can never return. I think it is that, for some reason, shriveled souls have come to prefer weeping and gnashing of teeth to true joy. Hell is a choice, and sometimes we opt for the pathetic smallness of our own wailing.

So, what is our hope? Our hope is Jesus, who spoke of the narrow road, died for all, and offers us the choice to respond in faith and love. The good news of life and faith is that we are not left to ourselves. We are given the ability to have our souls rejuvenated, to turn our souls around and seek a more solid life. This is, in fact, the story of Augustine himself, as told in his autobiography *The Confessions of Saint Augustine*. He discussed his sinful past and demonstrated the way out—confession and repentance—leading to a faith in Jesus.

The shriveled soul is a state familiar to all humans. No persons, with the exception of Jesus, can say that they have continually made solid choices in their life. Even Augustine, a saint of the church, fell short. The crucial difference between a shriveled and a solid soul is repentance.

In the Hebrew, "to repent" means to turn around. For instance, Jonah ran away from God. God's destination for Jonah was east toward Nineveh, but Jonah physically went the opposite direction, west toward Tarshish. The story of Jonah is how, with the help of a storm and a big fish, Jonah literally turned his life around to go back east. Life consists of a seemingly infinite sequence of moments in which we choose which direction we are going. Like Jonah, we must continually be willing to turn around and go in God's direction. Our souls depend on it.

This book is intended to be useful to people of all faiths and those with no faith, because an eternal lens and a focus on our direction or trajectory in life is helpful for all people. I am confident, though, that, when we reach heaven, Jesus will be on the throne. His death and resurrection are the pivotal moments for us and everyone we have ever met. Jesus said, "He who seeks shall find, he who knocks the door shall be answered" (see Matthew 7:7-8). I believe that all who truly seek heaven will find it in Jesus. As Augustine writes to God in *Confessions*, "Our hearts are restless until they find their rest in you."[8]

May we live lives where our choices lead toward heaven. In the chapters to come, our choices will become clearer as we look at daily struggles in which we are faced with the option between a more solid soul and a more shriveled soul. In part two, we will look at our souls in relationship with other souls. Marriages can either flourish or become pathetic, selfish shells of what could have been. Relationships with children can be either problems to solve or people with meaning and value for each other. Friendships can be bonds of beautiful honesty and dreaming or mere contacts that we spend time with. Souls connecting through marriage, family, and friendships should be relationships in which our souls become more and more solid. We are often so afraid of conflict and difference that we sometimes avoid a better path and let our souls atrophy.

In part three, we will look at how we go upward and onward, seeking new heights of life and hope. We will walk with Epiphanie, a friend of mine from Rwanda, as she takes an eternal look at orphans of genocide and believes that they can create a beautiful world around them. We will read the story of David Michel, who left ministry as a pastor to create opportunities for children and adults to live their best lives. We will end asking ourselves, "How can we structure our lives to create the most impact on ourselves and others in this world while we are here?"

Shriveled souls are real, but they are not inevitable.

PART TWO

Souls In Relationship

"The Bible knows nothing of solitary Christianity."

John Wesley

Our essential need for relationships is built into the very fiber of our being from the moment of our creation. God made us in God's image and called us good. The first point is that the nature of God is inherently relational. God, is in relationship at every moment: Father, Son, and Holy Spirit. If you ever wondered why you long to be loved and to love others, it is because we were made in the image of the one who loves perfectly and constantly. The second point is that for God, being in relationship with God's self was not enough. God created angels and dolphins, galaxies and sunflowers. God wanted friends, and so God made us.

Like God, we were made to be connected to others in deep and fulfilling relationships. The difficulty is that, unlike God, we are often bad at those relationships. There is no perfect marriage or friendship. There are no perfect parents or grandparents. At our best, we are flawed yet humble souls, continually seeking for our relationships to mirror the love that God has for us. These relationships shape our souls to love God and one another and thereby become more solid. At our worst, we lie, cheat, bully, manipulate, and damage others. That damage then radiates from one person to another in a vicious and cascading cycle of hell. What would our lives look like if our relationships, our marriages, families, and friendships took a better trajectory?

The following chapters are designed to help us become more solid souls by making our relationships better. In chapter four, we will look at marriages and what we can learn from failure. In chapter five, we will look at the relationship of parents and children and how every human of every age has a full-sized soul. In chapter six, we will look at friendships and how God can bind two souls together to live full and meaningful lives with or without the complications of sex. In chapter seven, we will look at the difficulty of being honest and living truly with ourselves and others.

Think about your own life and the relationships that fill it up. God made those relationships for you. Do you want those relationships to exist in a virtuous cycle of truth and love? It is what God hopes for you.

4 | Strengthen Your Marriage

I believe deeply in strong marriages. Biblically, a marriage is a union that is so sacred and important that the primary metaphor in Scripture is of the union between Christ and the Church. It is a connection forged in mutual submission so tremendous that it is the same love as Jesus's willingness to submit to death on the cross. My passion for strong marriages is grounded in both my own lived experiences as a husband and pastor and in watching my parents's marriage. Jenny Gomez, a licensed professional counselor who specializes in play therapy, has often said that what children need most is for their parents to have a strong and abiding marriage.[1] This is what I had growing up. I knew beyond a doubt that my parents loved each other and would sacrifice for each other. While I knew people who had been divorced and had come from divorced families, I was shocked and unprepared for the moment when my first marriage failed.

The summer before my senior year in college at the University of Kansas, I fell in love with a girl. She was smart, fun, and beautiful, and I was infatuated. We became friends at the end of our junior year. We met through the campus ministry that I helped lead. We stayed in touch through the summer; when she studied abroad in Paris, I met her there, and we became more than friends. By the time I returned home, the future seemed inevitable. We would date through senior year, get engaged, be married, and spend the rest of our lives together. My parents had met at KU. My grandparents had met at KU. It seemed natural that I would meet my wife at KU. We would organize our yearly travel schedules around March Madness, and we would cheer on the Jayhawks together.

Much of that happened. She moved out to North Carolina where I planned to attend seminary, and we got married the following summer. I was thrilled to have found my person, the "one." I imagined we would be together for better or worse, richer or poorer, in sickness and in health, and that we would love and cherish each other until we were parted by death. The next few years felt easy. In retrospect, too easy.

Less than three years later, my mom flew out to North Carolina, and together we removed my items from the townhouse where my wife and I had lived. My wife had already moved out. We packed the items into a U-Haul trailer, and my mom and I drove back to Dallas. I had called the church where I had been appointed to serve in ministry to let them know that my wife was not going to be joining me and that I hoped that they would still want me as a pastor even though I was in the middle of an impending divorce. Fortunately, I was to be at a church that would love me, care for me, and let me heal.

I moved into an apartment big enough, so that, if somehow my wife and I were to reconcile, she could move in with me, but not so big that it would be too much for just me. My mom and family moved me into my new apartment, and when they were done, I was left in the apartment alone, confronting one massive question: What happened?

I did not believe in divorce. It had never occurred to me that my marriage wouldn't last forever. What did I do wrong? And more important, how could I make sure that it would never happen again?

The Merging Of Souls

Marriage is a public and spiritual act binding two souls together. Marriage is best understood by paying attention to the difference between living together—cohabitation—and marriage. Over the last decade of my ministry, more and more people who had been living together for multiple years have come to me to be married. Rarely are their bank accounts merged before marriage, but their lives are so intertwined that separation would feel like a divorce without the title or lawyers. Mostly, they are afraid when they come to my office to plan the wedding and do premarital counseling that I am going to judge them. I always tell them some version of my own story of divorce to show them that I try not to judge people for decisions that they have already made. Living together is an understandable attempt to determine compatibility before the final step of marriage. Many of us, especially from the boomer generation to today, grew up in divorced families. Living together feels like a way of making sure that does not happen to us.

One of my primary goals in these conversations is to explain how their future marriage will be different from their past of living together. Marriage is a couple's public declaration of commitment, before God and a community of family and friends, that they will love and commit to each other for the rest of their lives. One way to say this is that marriage is about the merging of souls, who, for their time on earth, will be bound to each other. Living together, even for years, cannot simulate that kind of unity. The act of marriage—the uniting of souls—will always be an act of faith, even with months or years of a "trial run" under the belt.

Because marriage is always a leap of faith, it feels like a risk. This public declaration of love reminds me of the story of the Spanish conquistador Hernando Cortez who landed in Mexico. To solidify commitment and resolve disputes among his men, he burned the ships that could take them back to Spain.[2] Marriage is public. It is a legal and spiritual bond. Failure can be an embarrassment. I have seen family and friends in bad marriages, and it looks like they are imprisoned rather than rejoicing in a gift that fulfills them more than when they were single. Marriage has become both a Hallmark stereotype and a bogeyman. We desperately want good marriages, but we are paralyzed by our fear of what happens if things don't go well.

The problem with this thinking is that it is binary: all good or all bad. Marriages, like a person, are not all good or bad but rather a complicated mixture of decisions and life, which can become either better or worse. If we think about marriages in terms of souls, it changes the conversation. Souls can merge and grow together, or they can move apart or separate. In relationship, our souls are always doing one or the other. Marriages, which are composed of souls, are never static.

After my divorce, I discovered a marriage researcher named John Gottman. Gottman wrote the *New York Times* bestseller *The Seven Principles for Making Marriage Work*. It is not a religious book, but I always ask every couple that I marry to read it, along with Tim Keller's book *The Meaning of Marriage*.[3] Gottman's method of research was to put couples in an apartment for the weekend and monitor their interactions, including their words, body language, and facial expressions. He would then track them for years to see who remained married and who divorced. Over time, he developed the ability to predict divorce with a 90+ percentage accuracy.[4] The critical insight was that the primary predictor was not based on *what* the couple disagreed about, but rather *how* they disagreed. Unlike most of what I had thought previously, I realized that a good marriage is not simply about successful conflict resolution.[5] Having a great marriage is about treating the other person not as a problem but as an infinitely valuable soul. Gottman writes that "in the strongest marriages, husband and wife share a deep sense of meaning. They do not just 'get along.' They also support each other's hopes and aspirations and build a sense of purpose into their lives together."[6] This type of marriage is neither a Hallmark stereotype nor a bogeyman, but a gift. Marriage is the merging of two souls walking into an unknown future, hand in hand.

Divorced Persons Club

The greatest surprise to me when I moved back home after my divorce was how many people had been divorced and were willing to talk with me about it. Pastor friends that I have known my whole life took me out to breakfast and shared their personal journeys. It was as if there was a divorced person's club that I had never known existed. I am told that the same thing is true for alcoholics and those who have suffered from drug addiction. The joy for me was that I was not alone in my pain. I had the privilege of hearing other stories that sounded just like my own. These stories gave me hope that my divorce would somehow not ruin my life.

In the ten years since, I have come to believe that, while horrible and not what God originally intended, my divorce has become a gift. How could this be? How could something so horrible result in something good? I learned that I am more than my choices. God made me a soul, and souls can be redeemed. Years after my divorce, I chose to tell my congregation that I had been divorced. I was terrified that day. Would they still trust me? Would they like me after I told them that I had been a failure? I discovered the opposite. Counterintuitively, my honesty about my past failure made them trust me more. One church member said to me, "I liked listening to you before this sermon, but your vulnerability made me trust you as my pastor." Somehow, like Joseph, what we did was bad but God worked it for good.[7]

Statistics will tell you that this is not everyone's experience of divorce. John Gottman, for instance, notes that "some studies find the divorce rate for second marriages is as much as ten percent higher than for first-timers."[8] This fact should not surprise anyone; I know that I was in no shape to be married to anyone soon after my divorce. I had to change course, which is another way of saying, I needed to repent. In the preface to *The Great Divorce*, Lewis writes:

I do not think that all who choose wrong roads perish; but their rescue consists in being put back on the right road. A sum can be put right: but only by going back until you find the error and working it afresh from that point, never by simply *going on*. Evil can be undone, but it cannot 'develop' into good. Time does not heal it. The spell must be unwound, bit by bit, 'with backward mutters of dissevering power'—or else not. It is still 'either-or'.[9]

I had an either/or choice ahead of me. I could choose to dive into another relationship without changing my habits and thoughts, or I could choose a different trajectory.

When I chose to start dating again after more than a year, I attempted online dating. On match.com, one of today's popular sites for dating, there is a box on the profile page, which I came to call the "stat sheet." My dating stat sheet publicized a 5'11", 28-year-old divorced preacher. I was embarrassed, but it was all true, and I knew my future wife would see that stat before she knew anything else about me. Online dating was emotionally brutal, but it worked. After almost two years of online searching, my wife Becky accepted a first date with me, in part because she decided that she wanted to hear what happened. A 28-year-old divorced preacher would have to have a good story, she thought. If you know Becky, you know that Becky loves a good story!

I do not remember what I said to her as explanation for my divorce on that first night, but Becky listened to me struggle to be a better version of myself. While she too knows that divorce is not what God wants, she often says that she is better off, because she got "Arthur version 2.0." I attempted, in dating and our engagement, to avoid making the same mistakes with Becky that I did with my first wife. We got married in a snowstorm in Waco, Texas on March 2, 2014, four years after my first wife informed me that she was moving out. Those four years were difficult but soul-shaping. God leveraged that time to forge me into a better man, pastor, husband, and now father.

Do not misunderstand me. Divorce is not necessary to become a different person. I know people who are married to the same person all their lives and have discovered a 2.0 version of themselves along the way. What is necessary for every marriage (and every person) is for the relationship to be on a good trajectory. But how do you do that? You can't change your spouse, but you can change you, and, in that way, you can change the trajectory of your relationship.

Trajectory

When couples come to my office for premarital counseling, I have a ritual. I grab a sheet of paper and a pencil, and I present a graph that looks like this:

I tell couples something like this: "This is a graph of happiness over time. Everyone begins happy enough. Almost every bride and groom that I have ever known is happy on their wedding day. Now you might think that this is going to be the happiest day of your life, but I'm here to tell you that in a marriage done right, happiness only grows. Ideally, every day is the happiest day of your life because you are on an upward trajectory together.

Have you known married couples who looked happy and then suddenly got divorced? I want to explain that to you. You see, a great marriage and a marriage doomed to fail look pretty similar at the beginning. The novelty of being married is so much fun that, in the beginning, it gets you a long way, and, in general, you are happy. Here is how that looks after three years of marriage:

On the scale, the couples appear rather happy! But both joy and anger compound. And what was tiny in year three or four ends up on a trajectory that is vastly different from where it began. This is how I finish out the graph:

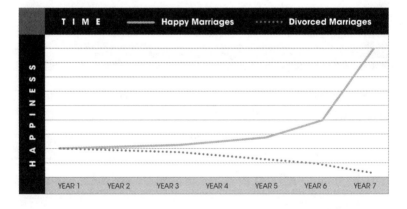

If you were to take a snapshot of time and simply look at happiness, both sets of couples would appear happy enough for the first few years. But when you pull back and look at the trajectory, it is rather clear where it is going. John Gottman's work has evolved to the point that he can look at the trajectory of a single conversation and determine whether it is moving in the right direction or the wrong direction. Still, not one single conversation makes or breaks a marriage. The success or failure of a marriage is about the cumulative effect of either care and devotion or neglect and difficulty. My understanding of the marriage trajectory comes not only from my own experience and counseling in ministry, but also from Gottman's description of what goes on as a marriage begins to fail. The sequence begins something like this:

1) *Conversations have a harsh startup.*
2) *The Four Horsemen of the Apocalypse appear:* Criticism, Contempt, Defensiveness, and Stonewalling.
3) *Flooding occurs.* Feelings appear which shut one or both partners down.
4) *Body language changes.* Couples fight or flee.[10]

This sequence is often repeated. I have had people in my office who are contemplating divorce ask me how John Gottman overheard their conversations in order to write his book. Gottman's progression described exactly the trajectory of their conversations.

As with all relationships, the damage done when a couple is in a negative spiral impacts everyone around them. Our next chapters are going to explore this same lens of life in regard to our relationships with our children, our friends, and our co-workers. We will pay attention to more than the snapshot of where we stand with our current relationships; we will ask: Where is the trajectory of each of our relationships headed?

Because souls are not static, relationships between souls never stay the same. If you ask a couple how their marriage is, they may respond honestly, saying, "Oh, it is about the same as it always has been." This has become for me a warning sign. Nothing remains steady. Souls (and relationships between souls) are always either growing or shriveling.

We begin the section on relationships with a chapter on marriage because marriage makes for an easy lens to see a fundamental truth about all relationships: if we are not nurturing our marriage, then it is decaying. A garden that is left unattended dies or is overrun by weeds. Muscles are either used or they atrophy. Souls are the same. Marriages, the merging of two souls into one entity, are the same. The biblical goal for marriage is for husband and wife to "become one flesh" (Genesis 2:24), which means that the success of each soul in a marriage is dependent upon the trajectory of that marriage and vice versa.

Like the graphs above, we should not look at a snapshot of our marital satisfaction—happiness, joy, or whatever word you choose to use for the left side of the axis—but we must recognize that we and our relationships are not static. Our relationships are continually being shaped. What feels like a tiny slide downward can compound quickly. I know that because that is how I felt about my first marriage. I was happy enough, so I assumed my wife was happy enough. Yet there is no such thing as "happy enough." We are either moving toward happiness or away from it. Toward joy or away from it.

My greatest flaw in my first marriage is that I ignored my relationship's trajectory. By the time I paid sufficient attention to my marriage, it was already gone. I looked only at the snapshot and thought, "I am happy enough." I did not pay attention to the direction that the marriage was going. Describing a different couple in his book, Gottman wrote words that could have applied to me:

"Although they still live together, they are leading lonely lives. They have become like ghosts, haunting the marriage that once made them both feel so alive."[11]

That was, in part, my fault. I resolved to do better next time.

Souls Are Not About The Big Things

Once Becky and I were married, I was so alert to our trajectory that I was a little too intense in making sure that I was doing everything that I needed to be doing for our marriage. Becky regularly would calm me down and remind me that she was not going to leave me, that I could just relax and enjoy being married to her. But it was difficult to relax when I was so convicted by my first marriage that what happened then must never happen to me again. Over time, I began to discover the truth about marriages. Tending to souls is most often not about the big things.

Marriages are complex and difficult because our souls are complex and difficult. As we have discovered, we often do not know what we want, and we cannot know the future. If we have no idea what will make us happy and satisfied now or in the future, how do we tend to our marriages and ensure that they are on the right trajectory? By caring for the other person's soul.

I have come to love the concept of a soul, because it encompasses every part of us. I pray and care for my wife, not just as a wife, but as a mother, a daughter, a friend, and someone with her own dreams and aspirations. In our first years of marriage, I tried to make sure that I was everything I could be for Becky, but there is no way that I could do that. Attempting to be everything to another person, trying to fill someone else's every need, is a recipe for disaster. I have learned that I can tend to my wife's soul by supporting and loving her in ways that allow her to be who she wants to be. Here is my mental checklist of the things that fill up her soul:

- *Girls's Weekends.* Becky loves to hang out with friends of hers for a day or two at a time, when they can sit and talk for hours and hours on end. It is neither difficult nor heroic for me to be alone with our children for a few days.
- *Coffee Shops.* Becky's happy place is to sit with a computer and work at a coffee shop for a few hours.
- *Date Nights.* Becky loves surprises. I try to surprise her with these whenever we get a chance.
- *Family Trips.* Becky loves the moment when we are in a car together as a family going somewhere, whether it is a day trip or a week-long vacation.

None of these are massive things, but I have come to know what my wife needs for her soul to be fulfilled. Every person's list will be different, but it is the attention to each other and the tending of each other's souls that makes all the difference.

Gottman describes how small these items of attention might be: "Comical as it may sound, romance actually grows when a couple is in the supermarket and the wife says, 'Are we out of bleach?' and the husband says, 'I don't know. Let me go get some just in case," instead of shrugging apathetically. . . . Couples that turn toward each other remain emotionally engaged and stay married. Those that don't eventually lose their way."[12] Notice that Gottman did not say that affairs or moving jobs or any other massive things caused the divorces in his study. Usually, it is our simple day-to-day habits that dictate the trajectory of our marriages. We tend to each other's souls through daily habits. I have learned that my marriage is dependent on whether I tend to Becky's soul, and she tends to mine.

On To Perfection

By the age of twenty five, I had been down the path of the four horsemen of the apocalypse with my first marriage. I experienced a negative trajectory in my life, and I did not want to be on it again. It took me a long time to be generous in my thoughts about my ex-wife, until I realized that the task for my soul was to repent of my own contributions to the failed marriage. She is in charge of her own soul, and I have come to wish her the best.

My life is a constant reminder that our past does not have to define us; we can be redeemed. As I write this, I am holding my nine-month-old daughter in my lap as a physical reminder of this redemption. My marriage to Becky is not perfect, but it is going in the right direction. It is on the way to perfection. Becky and I are on a spiritual trajectory that gives me excitement for the future.

When I was little, I thought very simply about my parents's marriage. It simply was. It seemed a fact, one of the immutable laws of the universe. As an adult, I have come to see their marriage as its own journey, a trajectory of life, love, and hope. My parents work on their marriage just like anyone else because they are two souls who have merged and are walking hand in hand into the future.

I have constantly thought about my marriage and this story during the year 2020, because I have had conversations with people who were terrified by the discovery in March that they were going to be quarantined with someone they were married to for weeks or months on end. I anticipated the consequences of quarantine and knew that the coronavirus may be the final nail in the coffin for a number of marriages that were already on the brink. During quarantine and COVID, you cannot distract or hide from a marriage that drains your soul rather than fills it.

My word of hope is this: You can become version 2.0 in your marriage. You do not need a new spouse to become a better version of yourself. If you are in a marriage that is not going well, redemption is possible, but it will require going in a different direction.

A new trajectory is always possible—in this life and the next.

5 | Full-Sized Souls

My first job in church service was to lead a young adult ministry, which was challenging because there were not many young adults. In fact, most of my job consisted of talking to parents of young adults who were convinced that I could successfully intervene with their uninterested adult children. Those conversations could have gone like this:

"Hello? Is this Arthur, the pastor for the young people?"

"Well, that is one part of my job. How can I help?"

"Fantastic. I need you to fix my son."

"Excuse me? What's going on? Can you help me understand?"

"Absolutely. My son has gone off the deep end. He is hanging out with people that I do not like, and he is not listening to me anymore. What do I do? I need your help! He will end up at college, and he will never come back, and who knows what he will do there."

"Okay, if he is still in high school, then what we need to do is get our youth pastor involved to see if we can't get him connected to the programs that we have here."

"We don't have time for that. I need this fixed before he goes to college!"

"Okay. When does he leave for college?"

"Two weeks. I need an intervention or something."

"Ma'am, I would love to help find some ways to help the two of you engage, but I have no idea how anything is going to change if he is leaving in two weeks."

Numerous times after calls like this, I thought, "What in the world could anyone do in such a short time frame? Even if I tried, how do I fix someone who doesn't want to be fixed?" After I became a parent, I began to understand that desire; I have wanted to "fix" my son or daughter when they have had tantrums or have refused to do things that are good for them. While toddlers are different than teenagers or young adults, the struggle to successfully guide children to become their best self is constant. One lens to help us reimagine this relationship is to understand that children are full-sized souls. Think about the people you valued when you were a child. They were probably people who spoke *to* you and not *about* you. They would often get down on your level and look you in the eye. They did not discount your feelings or say that you simply needed to get over yourself. They behaved as if you mattered. The truth is, they treated you as a valued person, a soul.

This is not a chapter on parenting strategies. I am not an expert on getting children to eat their entire dinner or on how to effectively convince teenagers to minimize time on social media. In the three years that I have been a parent, I have made plenty of mistakes and have called others who are experts in how to have a toddler and an infant under the same roof. Alongside my wife, I am doing the best I can with what I know to accomplish the short-term tasks of everyday life.

This is a chapter on who our children are. They are eternal beings of infinite worth. In between soccer practice, school, vacations, and bedtimes, we can get too focused on the strategies and systems of parenting. We compare grade point averages and growth charts, dream of schools and careers, all the while surviving the day-to-day needs of life. Sometimes we overlook one simple fact: our children already are full-sized souls. I wrote about this awareness in chapter one. Pastor and family-systems expert Kim Meyers says it this way:

> The first time we bring home a child, we look into this life
> that we are now responsible for and in that moment, we see

though the wholeness of this child. I personally was mes-
merized by my sleeping babies, overwhelmed by my screaming babies, and found such true joy in my giggling babies.
The problem with each feeling is exactly that . . . parenting
has an undercurrent of constant emotions. It can under-
whelm and overwhelm us at each stage. But when we focus
on the end goal of parenting to raise children who love
God and love their neighbor fully so that one day they can
show that love to others, this can reframe the emotional
moments and allow us to see our children as the full-sized
souls that they are from the very beginning.[1]

Tend To Their Souls

In the process of having children, Becky and I went through multiple fertility processes. In our second attempt at IVF (In Vitro Fertil-
ization), the process seemed to have worked. Dr. Sam Marynick, our
beloved fertility doctor, was looking at a sonogram of a seemingly
perfectly healthy child, and I asked an evidently pertinent question,
"So, can we stop worrying now?" He replied with a chuckle, "I don't
recommend you stop worrying until they are thirty!" As I retold this
story, laughing, with my mother, she replied, "What is so magical
about thirty? I'm still worried about all my kids who are well over
thirty!" I shared my mother's response with Dr. Marynick. He offered a medical explanation about how most mental and physical
disorders become evident by thirty years of age. My mother knew,
however, that there is much more to worry about than just the body
and mind. Parents should also tend to their children's souls.

In my role as the pastor of young adults, I discovered that parent's fears for their children are varied. Some parents want their
grown children to come back to church as an adult. Others are
hoping for grandchildren and ask if there is a subtle way to ap-

proach that conversation. Every parent and child relationship has its own pattern, and as I am generally in the same generation as their children, church members see me as a safe person with whom to have a conversation. They are afraid to broach the subject with their own kids.

I don't mind these conversations. In fact, I have come to love them, because it gives me a chance to talk with church members about their own hopes and dreams, especially those intertwined with their now adult children. Parents often struggle as their children gain independence; they often don't realize that they remain the largest influence in their grown children's lives. Love and care from a parent does not stop at age 18. Most children are still looking for guidance and direction. As children grow older, parenting becomes less about control and more about influence. Consider, for instance, this conversation with "Suzie," a typical church member:

"Arthur, I have a question. How do I get my son to come to church with me this weekend?" (Pastoral Pro Tip: any conversation in which someone asks for help in getting another person to do what they want is bound to be interesting. This setup deserves more questions.)

"Wow, Suzie. I need more information before I can answer that. Can you help me out? It isn't Mother's Day or something like that. Is this Sunday special?"

"Oh, no. I just want him to come to church."

"Okay. Does he ever go to church?"

"Well, yeah, but only when I bug him to."

"So, you know you can get him to church if you bug him. So, are you asking me how you can get him to come this Sunday? Or are you asking how you get him to come on his own accord on a regular basis?"

"That one! It is just that, one day, my son is going to get

married and have kids, and I want my grandkids to come to church."

"Well, have you ever had that conversation with him?"

"Not really."

When children are young, it is easy to control their activities, but the older they get, the less that concept works. You can still see in the conversation with "Suzie" that the patterns of control are deeply ingrained. The real conversation that she wishes to have is one about marriage, children, and the passing on of faith and values. The actual conversations between grown adults and their parents contains nagging and begging (control) more than it does conversation about identity, hopes, and dreams (influence). Those core values and dreams feel so vulnerable to discuss that we are tempted to bury them deep down and pray that the ones we love most will understand us by osmosis.

At its core, this is the challenge of parenting. While I do not yet have teenagers, Kim Meyers describes her changed relationship with her teenage boys like this:

> We have lost daily control and touch points, but if you build a relationship with your children that is faithful and has trust, every choice they make has your influence. This is what gives me the most peace in raising our teenage boys. I know that we are preparing them to leave our home and create their own place in the world. We know that the faith that we live by will help guide our children to claim their own faith.[2]

Kim is clear about her dreams for her children, years into the future, and this allows her to think with a longer-term lens. She has learned to prioritize influencing and nurturing their souls. The short-term needs are always overwhelming. It never feels like there is enough time to get to our fundamental hopes, and so, too often, we settle for something far less. Too many of us have had more blunt family conversations about which Mexican food restaurant has the best salsa than we have had about the very core portions of our souls.

As parents, we have focused so much on the short-term needs of food, clothing, friends, and sports that we sometimes forget that the children that we love and care for are not beings to control but eternal souls to nurture and tend. We must reclaim an eternal perspective of parenting.

How do you raise an eternal soul?

Connect, Don't Fix

In the year 2020, parenting felt different, to put it mildly. Schools, restaurants, and gyms shut down. Other venues were drastically limited, depending on the phase of the pandemic. Where once a family might have spent the spring at baseball tournaments, they had nothing but time to sit and look at one another. With no sports on television and no place to go, one parent told me that they rediscovered family game night. Other families spent new-found time biking, walking together, or eating together. A new sense of "family time" was restored from the hustle and bustle of pre-COVID, tech-savvy, twenty-first century life. These new changes came as a shock and challenge to many families who weren't used to spending that much time together—especially for those with young children and toddlers—but they were also learning opportunities about family, self-care, community, and what matters most.

When COVID hit in March, our household contained me, my wife, our two-and-a-half-year-old son Sam, and our five-month-old daughter, Ella Reece. Friends without children were boasting about how many television shows they had consumed and how great it was to have quiet nights. This was not our world. In February, the month before COVID hit, we had a world that supported us to be the best parents that we could be. Grandparents drove up at least once a month from Houston to stay and help out. Sam attended the preschool at our church, and we had a standing babysitter once a week to give us time to be with our small group of friends. Suddenly, all our support systems dropped. We were not alone in this. Parents across the world were thrust into being proctors for their children's online education. Parents were attempting to work from home while children were plopped in front of a television. Young families discovered how much we desperately need our various villages and communities to sanely raise and develop our children.

There were also some fantastic family moments that we were given during that time. I got to watch Ella Reece crawl for the first time. I missed that moment with Sam because I was at work. Sam got to join me for some work-related video conference meetings. We want on family walks, had lunch together most days, found a favorite fishing spot, set up shop in our front yard, met neighbors, and eased into a much slower pace. But over time, the continual day-to-day grind wore on us. Becky and I would put the children to sleep and then have just enough time to pick up, do the dishes, and reset the house for it to be destroyed again the next day. We entered true survival mode.

Survival mode is complicated. It is the reality and curse of parenting. From the moment a baby comes home from the hospital, there is a never-ending list of tasks to accomplish. COVID took the normal survival mode of parenting and made it relentless. As my wife and her friends communicated through daily texting threads, one voice began to bring them some perspective. A psychologist from New York whose Instagram handle is "@DrBeckyatHome" started doing Instagram stories. Night after night as we would go to bed, my wife would look at me and say, "You have to listen to this."

Two themes resonated with tired parents on the site:

1) **It is okay to be in survival mode.** *None of us has ever parented through a pandemic before.* In difficult trials, it is a relief to have an expert say that it is okay to struggle day to day. We had been second guessing our decisions throughout COVID. Do we let our children watch television? How much is too much? What about play dates with friends? New and overwhelming questions were constant in 2020, and it was necessary to hear that we are doing the best that we can.

2) **Connect, don't fix.** If you have the choice between connecting with your child or fixing their behavior, connect rather than fix. Dr. Becky says, "We want our kids to associate us with being with them in their tough times. This association both strengthens our relationship with our child and helps a child build resilience. Pretty good bang-for-your-buck."[3]

The first point was a great reminder, but it was this second point that resonated most with us. In one of her Instagram stories, Dr. Becky wrote a short sentence about connection: "When your children are grown and you can no longer discipline them, all you have is your connection."[4] The truth is, that is what souls are made for—connection. We are made to connect with one another, not fix one another. That toddler who hits while struggling to express frustration is not something that needs fixing, but a soul who needs connection. As a pastor, this is what I was trying to tell parents every time they called and asked how they could fix their children. Start with connection. If you must choose between connection and control, always choose connection.

The Family Trajectory—Connect Through Values

Family dynamics are never static, even if every time an extended family gets together, it feels like everyone has the same conversations every year. Imagine the changes that have happened in people's lives within the course of a year: jobs gained or lost, trips taken, hopes realized, dreams dashed. The only reason it feels like nothing ever changes is that we typically ask the same surface questions: "How are your kids?" "Fine." "Work?" "Same." Is that really all that has taken place within the year? It can't be. We have simply chosen to maintain relationships without connection.

Like the conversation on marriage, one consistent flaw in thinking about our relationships comes from looking at them as a snapshot rather than a trajectory. As parents and people with ongoing relationships, we need to be setting up the kind of shared values and communication that will ensure ongoing connection. The goal is not simply to connect, but rather to set up and live into patterns that offer continual, meaningful connection. Think about the best conversations you have ever had in your life, the ones where you connected deeply on topics that set your soul on fire. Because we are not machines, but souls, we have the privilege of having our souls resonate with other souls.

If you are raising a young child, do you want the conversations with your children to consist of one-word answers when they are in their thirties? I have been told that this may happen at some point in every child's development, somewhere around the teenage years, but that they often grow out of it. I have learned that they do not always grow out of it. Instead, it depends on the type of long-term connection you have been able to create. If we are thinking about our long-term dreams, the purpose is not simply for a single snapshot of time, but for something meaningful that can grow.

A few years ago, my wife and I started doing a family retreat every spring. We have an intentional weekend every year where we set up time to talk about the things that matter most in our lives. We created a set of written family values that we edit every year. Each year, we look at our values and evaluate how we did at holding to them or not, allowing us to either set new goals or recommit to the ones that we set previously. Starting this next year, we will bring Sam into some of those conversations.

This concept is an expanded version of something my parents enacted with me as a child. Every year, toward the end of December, my parents would sit down and show us a spreadsheet that displayed our charitable giving for the year. They would point to the tithe that we would make to the church, hiding the actual number so we remained ignorant of their salary at such a young age. They would then say, "We have set aside $XXXX.XX to give away this year, and we are going to make that decision as a family. Where do you feel called to give it?" Even though we were young and in elementary school, my parents were connecting with us on crucial questions about our family's collective values and goals.

My brother has kept this tradition with his children. His oldest daughter is now old enough to understand the question, and so he modified the process to give her a certain number of quarters. Together they talked about how to divvy them up. Each quarter represents a percentage of their charitable giving above and beyond their tithe. Already, their family is including their young daughter in the crucial question of value and connecting over core questions of identity and purpose.

This is why I feel strongly about having children sit throughout church services with their parents. The weekly practice of connecting during music, prayers, and preaching is a regular habit of sharing in the core questions of meaning and purpose. Even if the sermon isn't great or the music is lacking, the purpose of weekly worship is not about what any one person gets out of it; it is a shared connection of meaning and purpose. This sets up a different trajectory. Too often, parents give their children veto power over whether they go to church each week or not. This is backward thinking. These parents are thinking of the short-term need of surviving that week, rather than the long-term strategy of building a family that shares values, purpose, and meaning.

I am sure that some reading this feel like that time has passed them. You may have grown children whom you can no longer coerce into going to church. You may be asking, "What if I have already messed up?" The great news is that it is never too late. Seek true and meaningful connection. You and those you love are not things to be fixed, but souls to connect with. The time for doing that is never over.

Problem Solving Versus Soul Thriving

When I was growing up, my parents allowed me to watch only two television channels: PBS and the Discovery Channel. I remember *Sesame Street* and shows about sharks, but I loved Mr. Rogers. After watching a documentary about Mr. Rogers, I have been thinking deeply about Mr. Rogers's value to my generation. He feels like our only modern saint. I loved him. Mr. Rogers treated children differently from most people. He treated us as if we mattered and could make decisions. Frankly, he treated us as if we had souls. As a Presbyterian minister, he knew that, even if we were small, we had full-sized souls.

As a new parent, I have read books about how to do parenting well. With a baby, I read about how to get infants to sleep through the night. As we approached toddler phase, I took a parenting strategy class based on the concepts in the book *Love & Logic.*[5] I will continue to study and research strategy books, because there is a desperate need for parents to discover practical ways to survive and raise healthy and happy children. Parenting books and Instagram accounts are a resource that we can incorporate into who we are and who we want to be. Kim Meyers says:

> When I teach a parenting class, I always tell people, this book is black and white, but life is colorful. Take these techniques and lessons and incorporate them into your family to make you a better parent, not a different person.[6]

Parenting is the gift and challenge of shepherding a full-sized soul through the physical, emotional, and spiritual developments of life. Humans are not given a fully developed brain until they are well into their twenties, and yet they have a soul before they are born, and dreams and hopes by the time they are 2 years old. The people that I valued growing up—including my parents—were the ones who cared about me rather than trying to fix or manage me. As children, we were not problems to be solved or managed, but souls to help thrive.

I believe in God and heaven for countless reasons, but two moments that I will never forget are the ones where I held my children in my hands for the first time. How did parenting go from marveling at the miraculous infinite gift at birth to survival strategy sessions? We must have a better way of thinking about parenting, even if we understand that survival is part of our challenge. We will discover in the next two chapters that one secret to thriving in our relationships with friends, colleagues, enemies, and bosses is to remember that what is true of you and your family is also true of others. You have never met a mere mortal. We are all infinite souls who need to think about how we approach all of our relationships.

The Nursing Home Question

The cycle of parenting often ends with children taking on the roles of caretaker and decision-maker for their parents. In my own family, one grandmother developed Alzheimer's Disease and required skilled care for her final years. My other grandmother remained lucid and wise, living alone in her own home until she was 96. In both situations, their children were required to step in and help make decisions in their parents's lives to some degree. One day, I anticipate my wife and I filling that task for our parents, and one day—God willing—Sam and Ella Reece will do that for us. I once had a friend tell me that he needed to be a good parent, because one day, his children will be the ones deciding which nursing home he will go to. It is a helpful reminder that the way that I care for my children might become the way that they care for me.

What kind of relationship do you want to have when your children are planning elder care for you? Do you want your child to be focused on money or convenience? Or focused on loving and caring for you and your soul? Everything that we can do to lengthen our vision and imagine something closer to eternity makes our decision-making and choices better. The way that we lead and parent helps inform the souls of our children. Do we want our children to have solid or shriveled souls? I pray that, when my time comes for nursing-home care, Ella Reece and Sam will take time to connect with me and not "fix" me. I pray that they make decisions with care and compassion, always seeking what is best for Becky and me. I pray that they see us as eternal souls. If they do, even a nursing home could end up being heaven on earth.

6 | Love ≠ Sex

We were not made to be alone. In the story told in Genesis 2, God creates a man and then decides that a man alone is not a good thing: "It is not good for the man to be alone. I will make a helper suitable for him" (v. 18). God then invites the man to name the animals—livestock, birds, and wild animals—but none of them is suitable to be a full partner. So God creates a woman. The second chapter of Genesis ends with this set of comments: "That is why a man leaves his father and mother and is united to his wife, and they become one flesh. Adam and his wife were both naked, and they felt no shame" (Genesis 2:24-25). Of course, this moment where nakedness wouldn't produce shame was limited. First Eve and then Adam eat the forbidden fruit and cover themselves. From this moment on, relationships between people are irrevocably changed and different. Our relationships became sexualized.

Love and sex are two very different concepts. Sex is a beautiful gift from God intended for the covenant of marriage, which also includes a deep and abiding friendship. Sex outside of that covenant is the infiltration of the forbidden into what is otherwise a pure relationship. Since our undoing in Genesis 3, we have misunderstood and sexualized many of our relationships. Every relationship should have love. Not every relationship should include sex. That point should be self-evident. We have parents, siblings, children, co-workers, bosses, friends, acquaintances, and people with whom we interact for many other reasons.

In fact, almost every relationship in our lives is (or should be) free of sexual desires, tension, and acts. The television show *Friends* highlighted this effectively in an episode where Joey and Chandler somehow get free pornography channels on television. The plot line, which aired in March 1998, couldn't have happened even a few years later, as pornography became free and easy to access on computers and then cell phones.[1] But Joey and Chandler are ecstatic about their discovery and afraid that they might lose this sexualized storyline constantly playing in their apartment. So they never turn the television off. That is, not until they discover that watching porn does something to their view of the world and their neighbors:

> *Chandler:* Hey.
> *Joey:* Hey.
> *Chandler:* I was just at the bank, and there was this really hot teller, and she didn't ask me to go do it with her in the vault.
> *Joey:* Same kind of thing happened to me! Woman pizza delivery guy come over, gives me the pizza, takes the money, and leaves!
> *Chandler:* What? No, "Nice apartment, I bet the bedrooms are huge?"
> *Joey:* No! Nothing!
> *Chandler:* You know what? We have to turn off the porn.
> *Joey:* I think you're right.[2]

Joey and Chandler make the right decision to turn the television off for a few moments, and then decide that they prefer the more sexualized reality. Even though they know that it messed with their everyday interactions with other people, they turn the porn back on. This is an accurate description of the broken world in which we live and raise our children. We know we are messed up, but we often keep doing the things that mess up our friendships. We have lost our understanding of what true friendship really is. Consider *When Harry Met Sally,* the quintessential movie about two friends discussing whether men and women can be just friends without a sexual component. Spoiler alert: they end up together. The original script did not include the two of them getting together. Instead, they "meet each other years later and walk their separate ways."[3] It is almost as though Hollywood decision makers believed that sexualized relationships were the only ones that we would believe in. Or that would sell.

The problem with our lack of imagination around friendship is that we can have solid souls without having sex. Lots of people have done it. Look at Paul in the New Testament! But we cannot have solid souls without relationships and community. When Jesus is asked, "What is the greatest commandment?" he replies:

'Love the Lord your God with all your heart and with all your soul and with all your mind.' This is the first and greatest commandment. And the second is like it: 'Love your neighbor as yourself.' All the Law and the Prophets hang on these two commandments (Matthew 22:37-40).

Loving your neighbor is the basic framework for friendship. Love is greater than sex. Love is one soul choosing to engage and be vulnerable with another soul. Sometimes in my preaching and teaching, I have made a significant error, preaching one sermon about marriage for those who are married and another sermon about friendship for those who are single. The error was implicitly talking as if friendship were limited for those who are not married. This chapter is for everyone. This chapter is to help us understand that love from one soul to another is not to be limited to romantic relationships. If you are in a romantic relationship, you still need friends. If you are single, you need friends. The second greatest commandment cannot be fulfilled alone. Our goal is to reclaim some portion of that moment in the garden of Eden, or—to continue the story of Joey and Chandler—to find the true purpose of friendship, one that makes us want to turn the television off.

Iconic Friendships

What stories define the types of friendships you want to have? *Sex and the City* with the foursome of Carrie, Samantha, Charlotte, and Miranda? Or a duo like Patrick Stuart and Ian McKellen? What places represent the friendships that you respect, a coffee shop like in the television show *Friends*? Or a school where Zach and AC Slater might hang out in *Saved By the Bell*? Aside from pop culture, think about your closest friends who have passed the test of time. How did you actually become friends?

My best friend in college was a guy named Josh. He was from a small town called Sterling, Kansas, and we lived on the same floor our freshmen year at the University of Kansas. We became friends long before basketball started, but something between us clicked. Our friendship moved seamlessly from "Do you want to hang out this weekend?" to "What are we doing this weekend?" My best friend in Dallas became a guy named Drake. He is a member at my church, and he came to talk about faith and life. We ended up golfing together most weekends. I am his witness to a 427-yard drive. He drove over the green on a par 4, and I have not yet beaten him head-to-head in a game of golf. But it doesn't matter, because something else happened with Josh and me in college, and with Drake and me as adults. We became friends. Deep friends. Our souls resonated with each other. They have my back, and I have theirs.

Becky and I have discovered in our marriage that great friendships are necessary for thriving. A few months before we got engaged in the spring of 2013, we joined a small group of other couples and gathered to eat food, read the Bible, and share our lives each week. Most of us did not know one another well before that day, but over seven years, these people have become family. They have been a part of our marriage journey, our fertility journey, and are helping to raise our children with care, love, and support. We cannot imagine doing life without this group of friends.

What happens, exactly, when people find that they are willing to sacrifice for others, no questions asked?

One iconic story of friendship in the Bible is the bond between Jonathan and David, men who should have been rivals and instead became best friends. Jonathan was the son of King Saul. By normal standards, he should have been the next king, except according to scripture, King Saul had angered God, and God sent the prophet Samuel to anoint a new king in secret. That new king was a young shepherd boy by the name of David, who would soon receive acclaim and glory for defeating the giant Goliath and for his military successes against the Philistines. In due time, David would marry the king's daughter and would be loved by the people. In a normal Hollywood storyline, David and Jonathan would be rivals and enemies. But instead, the opposite happened:

> After David had finished talking with Saul, Jonathan became one in spirit with David, and he loved him as himself. From that day Saul kept David with him and did not let him return home to his family. And Jonathan made a covenant with David because he loved him as himself. (1 Samuel 18:1-3)

"One in spirit" is very different from the goal for Adam and Eve. Genesis 2 says that the goal of husband and wife is to be bound "in one flesh." The iconic story of friendship in First Samuel has Jonathan and David bound in one spirit. Some translations gloss over the actual concept discussed in the original text. The word regularly repeated in these verses is *soul.* Here is the same passage in the King James version, which retains the regularly repeated word in the original Hebrew:

> And it came to pass, when he had made an end of speaking unto Saul, that the soul of Jonathan was knit with the soul of David, and Jonathan loved him as his own soul. And Saul took him that day and would let him go no more home to his father's house. Then Jonathan and David made a covenant, because he loved him as his own soul.

No wonder the story of David and Jonathan is such an iconic image of friendship in Scripture. They are bound together, not by flesh, but by spirit. What an unbelievable vision for what friendship is! It is two (or more) souls who have chosen to bind themselves to one another. Such a connection is contagious. I love watching true friends engage with one another. Their souls are bound to one another, and they are filled with joy in their connection. This is our optimal goal, to love someone else as much as our very own soul. That concept is not limited to sex and marriage; those kinds of friendships should be cultivated and sought throughout our lives.

Holy Friendships Ask More

When we think about our most lasting friendships, they are often forged in difficult times: school, combat, work, and so forth. In the fall of 2020, I officiated the funeral for a marine, infantry platoon leader 1st Lt. Daniel Patrick Woulfe. It was an intensely emotional moment as Woulfe's ninth-grade son stood up to speak about his dad's faith and integrity. The speech from Woulfe's friend and Marine Corps brother, Major Mike Stambaugh, had something in particular to say about friendship and the Marines. Mike wanted the congregation to know that a marine, while certainly lethal, operates out of love for country, but particularly love for the brothers that are by his side in uniform.

Mike's speech for his friend gave me a lens to understand something significant about friendship. It rarely comes easy. The men and women whom I have known to have served in the military forged lasting bonds with one another, because they went through extremely difficult challenges together. Close bonds are rarely formed when things are easy. There is a sociological reason that communities throughout history, such as fraternities and sororities, have initiation periods that are extremely difficult. This is so that the newcomers to the organization will bond and forge deep ties with their peers. Think about the deep friends that you have. It is likely that they are connected to you through some moment(s) of serious effort. My friendship with Josh was born out of the difficulty of our first year of college when we were figuring out who we were. My friendship with Drake came out of a moment when I was going through a divorce, and I needed community and a regular golfing partner. Our small group at church connected largely because we all made the commitment to gather every single week out of the year and share a meal together. When our families began to have children, we paid for babysitters or had one family take care of our children every Tuesday night, so that we could gather in our small group. The effort required was a part of the secret sauce that made these friendships more lasting.

The reason that friendship is such a difficult thing to create as we get older is that the ready-made difficulties and insecurities of middle school, college, boot camp, or internships that bond people together are more difficult to find. As adults, we have trouble making deep friendships because we never treat anyone as more significant than an acquaintance. Dr. L. Gregory Jones, who happens to be my uncle and the dean of Duke Divinity School, has a framework for what "holy friendships" should look like. Holy friends, he says, do three things:

1) *Holy friends challenge the sins we have come to love.*
2) *Holy friends affirm the gifts we are afraid to claim.*
3) *Holy friends help us dream dreams we otherwise would not dream.*[4]

These are not standard expectations of normal friends. Any single one of them might be reserved for maybe the closest of friends. The first task asks a friend to call us out for things that we would rather not have called out. The second task gives us courage to be more of who God has made us to be. The third task helps set us off on a brand-new course that will change our life. How can we even conceive of moving from a surface-level happy hour with co-workers to this type of friendship?

As I was leaving the funeral for Lt. Dan Woulfe, a friend and church member stopped me in the parking lot. He was several decades older than Dan. He said, "If I had one person who was able to stand up and talk about me like Dan's friends and family talked about him, I would be lucky." I can name people who have been like Dan Woulfe to me. They have called me out when I needed to be called out. They have affirmed me when I couldn't affirm myself. And they have set me on a new course to forging a more solid soul. By God's grace, I know people like that in my life.

I recommend not starting your holy friendship by engaging first in "calling someone out." If anyone begins by challenging the sins I have come to love, then I will likely not listen to them again. But there is a fundamental point here about friendship. Holy friendship is difficult. It is hard to take the first step toward true, deep, intimate friendship. But the challenge to creating new and lasting friends cannot rest merely in someone else's hands. I could sit in my home waiting for someone to reach out to be the kind of friend that I need, or I could imagine that God is using this moment to ask me how I can be the friend that they need.

Another way to consider holy friendship is to paraphrase Jesus's Golden Rule, "Do to others as you would have them do to you" (Matthew 7:12), which might be rewritten, "Be the friend that you wish someone to be for you."

The Cost Of Friendship

In the biblical story of Jonathan and David, as their friendship grew, so did the king's hatred for David. David had been anointed king over Israel privately but had continued to serve Saul faithfully. Everyone in the country sensed that David had the blessing from the Lord, and they so loved him that it angered the king. Jonathan was in a difficult spot. His best friend, who had a competing claim to the throne, was at risk of being killed by his father. In one particularly tense moment, David is convinced that Saul is about to kill him, and so David and Jonathan devise a plot to figure out what to do. Jonathan becomes a spy against his father and discovers that his best friend's life is in danger. After Jonathan gives David the message that betrays his father, this is what happened:

> David got up from the south side of the stone and bowed down before Jonathan three times, with his face to the ground. Then they kissed each other and wept together—but David wept the most.
>
> Jonathan said to David, "Go in peace, for we have sworn friendship with each other in the name of the Lord, saying, 'The LORD is witness between you and me, and between your descendants and my descendants forever.'" Then David left, and Jonathan went back to the town (1 Samuel 20:41-42).

Jonathan and David would meet only one other time before Saul and Jonathan would die in battle at the hands of the Philistines.

Yet, in their last conversation, Jonathan once again takes a different path from that of his father:

> While David was at Horesh in the Desert of Ziph, he learned that Saul had come out to take his life. And Saul's son Jonathan went to David at Horesh and helped him find strength in God. "Don't be afraid," he said. "My father Saul will not lay a hand on you. You will be king over Israel, and I will be second to you. Even my father Saul knows this." The two of them made a covenant before the LORD. Then Jonathan went home, but David remained at Horesh (1 Samuel 23:15-18).

Jonathan told David that he would take second place; the rightful heir was willing to revoke his claim to the throne to make way for his friend. If you have either read or watched *Game of Thrones* or read history, this is not a standard gesture. Both fiction and non-fiction are littered with stories of kings killing anyone who has a valid claim to the throne, and yet here in the Scriptures is a different story, one that indicates the significance of David's and Jonathan's friendship. The original covenant by David ensured that their souls would be bound to each other. Jonathan loved David as his own soul, and in doing so, he demonstrated the solidity of his soul. He chose friendship and love over dominance and power. David's life and trajectory, and therefore the life and trajectory of Israel, was due to the humility and friendship of Jonathan. It was a holy friendship.

Sacred, Neither Discarded Nor Infatuated

In the Scriptures, *holiness* means set apart and cared for. Priests among the Israelite people were set apart as a special group who would intentionally care for the community and their relationship with the Lord.

Holy friendships, then, are the ones we have intentionally set apart and made sacred. This could be through a commitment like marriage (married people should be holy friends with each other); but notice that Jonathan and David were bound not through flesh but through their souls. They did not make a covenant of marriage but rather a covenant of friendship. They took the time to say specifically that they would value the other person, binding their souls in friendship, no matter what came next.

How many friends do you have that fit into this category? Would you be like Jonathan was for David? Would someone be that kind of friend for you? A soul becomes more solid through interactions with friends like this. Gary Thomas wrote a book entitled *Sacred Marriage,* with the subtitle "What If God Designed Marriage to Make Us Holy More Than to Make Us Happy?" This has been a best-selling book with more than a million copies sold. I have read the book and have used it. But I bring it up in this chapter on friendship because it is not the sexual component of marriage that should make us holy and not merely happy; it is the friendship component of marriage. Any relationship that binds two souls together in a way that can challenge sins we love, affirm gifts we are afraid to claim, and help us dream dreams we otherwise would not dream is one that will make us into more solid souls.

To be our best selves, we need relationships with other people that are sacred. Many relationships are stunted because we are infatuated with shiny things (money, sex, and so forth). Others atrophy because we do not give them enough attention. If holiness means to be "set apart" and cared for, then the opposite is to be common or ordinary. Only extraordinary friendships, ones that get to the core of our being, are sacred and help us become more solid.

Mephibosheth

True friendship that is formed from souls that are bound together leaves a lasting impact on those around them. After Saul and Jonathan die in battle with the Philistines, David asks in 2 Samuel 9:1, "Is there anyone still left of the house of Saul to whom I can show kindness for Jonathan's sake?" He is informed that there is a young man who cannot walk, Jonathan's son, Mephibosheth. David contacts him and says, "Don't be afraid . . . for I will surely show you kindness for the sake of your father Jonathan. I will restore to you all the land that belonged to your grandfather Saul, and you will always eat at my table" (v. 7).

The beauty of holy friendship is that it lasts eternally. It lasted past Jonathan's life on earth and will last in heaven when Jonathan and David are able to embrace as friends again. Too many relationships on earth are cheap and over almost as soon as they begin. They are often not bound with the kind of love that binds together souls. In our world today, we have limited love to romantic love, but the love that Jonathan showed David during his lifetime and that David showed Jonathan after his death was more powerful than many marriages.

7 | Truth Will Set You Free

My brother-in-law likes to tell a bad joke: "What do a youth pastor, an accountant, and an FBI agent have in common?" The trick answer is that they are all attributes of my brother-in-law![1] Reese graduated with a master's degree in accounting and began working for a major international accounting firm. He was still determining what his long-term career would be and chose to pursue his childhood dream of becoming an FBI agent. With the way the government works, however, that process would take a very long time. So, Reese quit his job in accounting and became a youth pastor. One day, he received his call to join the FBI and pursue his dream. At Quantico, the location of FBI agent training center, the director of the training program was asking people about their past and came to Reese:

"What did you do before coming here?" he asked.

"Well, sir, I was a youth pastor," Reese replied.

The director was dumbfounded and shouted to the whole room: "You know why I love this place? We have everyone! We have military, we have lawyers, we have accountants, and even a *&$*&% youth pastor!" While the epithet was unwarranted, the point was fair. What do a youth pastor and an FBI agent have in common? Simple. They work with people, and they seek truth. But as Reese came to discover, as he worked in the FBI, received training, and worked cases as an FBI negotiator, truth can be a difficult thing.

Just a year or so after his job as a youth pastor, telling students how much God loves them, Reese found himself sitting across the table from a woman whose 19-year-old, live-in boyfriend had just bought a grenade off the "dark web." In case you are interested in doing the same, you should know that the seller was the FBI pretending to sell explosives. Sitting across from this young woman,

Reese said, "First, I can tell that you are lying. Second, I know you know more than you are saying. Third, I can also tell that this is crushing you. To be free of this crushing feeling, you need to tell the truth." While this is not always a strategy that a lawyer might recommend to a client, it is an effective strategy for an FBI agent, because truth is a part of our basic human make-up. We were made to live authentic lives. Holding back the truth imprisons us or, as Reese told that young woman, it crushes us.

In the last chapter, we talked about the loss in Genesis 3 when Adam and Eve disobeyed, discovered they were naked, and hid themselves from God. The story reveals a fundamental truth: we have been covering up our true selves for almost all our lives. Everyone has something to hide and something of which they are ashamed. When he entered the FBI, Reese believed this, but in his years in the bureau, he saw more than any of us wanted to see. His first case involved sitting across from a woman whose husband had been arrested for child molestation. His job was to ask questions about the minute and tragic details of their intimate lives. We are not all that broken, but we are all living in a world that is that broken. Social media and cell phones bring that world into our very homes and lives. How do we deal with this kind of deep brokenness?

In Ephesians, when Paul is trying to prepare the church in Ephesus for facing this type of brokenness, he writes this:

> Put on the full armor of God, so that you can take your stand against the devil's schemes. For our struggle is not against flesh and blood, but against the rulers, against the authorities, against the powers of this dark world and against the spiritual forces of evil in the heavenly realms (Ephesians 6:11-12).

There is something difficult and broken in our world and in each of us. You may find it hard to believe in the devil, but it was clear to me, as I stood in concentration camps in Germany and genocidal killing fields in Rwanda, that there are spiritual forces of evil. The premise of this book maintains that you and I are more than mere flesh and blood. Perhaps this explains why we can choose either sacrificial acts of love or conceive and enact horrid atrocities upon others. Our life as either "immortal horror" or "everlasting splendor" (as C. S. Lewis puts it) begins in the here and now.[2] The impetus of choosing which path we will take can be as simple as the conversation that Reese had with that young woman. The question is, will we choose to live in truth?

God is the only one to hold absolute truth (Jesus said, "I am the . . . truth," John 14:6), and for us to become solid souls we must continually seek to live according to the truth that is both within and beyond us. We must be honest with ourselves about our own internal self, our actions and desires, and we must wisely and vulnerably share that truth with others. The first piece of armor that Paul describes in Ephesians is a belt of truth (Ephesians 6:14). As Jesus said, "The truth will set you free" (John 8:32).

Will we be true to ourselves and others?

Experience, Not Truth, Is Relative

What is truth? Entire divisions of philosophy have been dedicated to this question. During Jesus's pre-execution interview, the Roman Prefect Pontius Pilate asked Jesus that same question. Here is a portion of their interaction in the Gospel of John:

> "You are a king, then!" said Pilate.
>
> Jesus answered, "You say that I am a king. In fact, the reason I was born and came into the world is to testify to the truth. Everyone on the side of truth listens to me."

"What is truth?" retorted Pilate (John 18:37-38a).

Here you have Jesus, God, attesting that there is truth. Yet the elite ruler Pontius Pilate scoffs at the notion. Scripture says that Pilate did not wait for a response but left to go and deal with the Jews who were accusing Jesus, claiming that there was no basis for a charge against the accused. Pilate even offers to send Jesus back to them, as it was a Roman custom to release one Jewish prisoner each year at the time of the Passover. Note this moment. Pilate found no cause for a charge, but that was not enough to free Jesus. Truth, in Pilate's mind, remained relative, nonexistent, or ultimately unimportant.

Our world has resorted to Pilate's derision, choosing to reject the idea that truth can exist in the world. Truth, in Pilate's understanding, was relative. Over time, we have learned to question everything as Pilate did two thousand years ago, to the point of questioning reality or truth itself. We have even come to a time when there is consideration that we are "post-truth," which was the Oxford Word of the Year in 2016.[3] What it means is that we have often conflated reality with our experience of reality. I prefer Martin Gurri's explanation in *The Revolt of the Public and the Crisis of Authority in the New Millennium*:

> I want to make my terms very clear. I don't believe reality is malleable, variable, or constructed. Reality is as unyielding as a policeman's club. Unlike that club, however, the *shared* reality of 320 million persons can't be experienced directly: it's mediated. For the last century and a half, the elites, and even more the institutions they manage, have been the arbiters of mediated certainty and truth.[4]

Authorities and institutions, such as government, education, media, and healthcare once determined what was "true" and what was not; however, that role was found wanting as soon as we could Google an answer, share an unedited image, or express our own feelings on social media. The faculty of knowing truth was once claimed only by elites like Pontius Pilate, who arbitrated "certainty." Now knowledge of truth is claimed by everyone. Dietary guidelines once told us fats were bad and carbohydrates were good. Now we are told that fats are good and carbohydrates are bad. Some will say that this is how science works. Bad information gets replaced with good. That may be, but this underestimates the consequences to our world about what *truth* is. If the Centers for Disease Control or our health organizations say one thing is true only later to say that something else is true, this dichotomy diminishes the concept for us that there is any such thing as truth. And if there is no such thing as truth, then we begin to believe that reality itself is malleable or constructed, when, instead, our reality was created by a Creator.

We do not get to choose the universe in which we live. The only question is what to do with the reality we have been given.

The rise of phrases like "my truth" or "his truth" or "her truth" hides from us that we are subject to a truth beyond ourselves. While this phrasing has seemed useful as a way of articulating underlying emotions and experiences that are particular to one person, it does so by obscuring reality and, therefore, the need to change. "This was my fault," I told myself when someone did not like me. That was "my truth." Everything that person did and said seemed to fit this *truth*, but it was only because I was cherry-picking the facts and data that fit my own, internal conclusion.

I believe this penchant for us to "create" our own truth explains a large portion of middle-school angst. My brother came home every day complaining of a boy who did not like him. That boy, meanwhile, went home and told his mother that my brother did not like him. They each had constructed their own "truth," except none of it was truth at all. It was merely their perception of truth. Their experiences were relative. The truth was that they were obscuring the reality of their relationship by telling themselves stories. In business, obscuring reality means losing a lot of money, and so there are tools to evaluate whether a conclusion should be acted upon.[5] One of the greatest dangers for a company—or a person—is to take an action based on the stories we tell ourselves rather than examining the underlying reality. Of course, just because we have the tools to fight misperceptions doesn't mean that we always utilize them.

So, how do we determine whether something is an underlying reality or the result of our impressionable emotions? We begin by acknowledging that many of our choices are based on momentary emotions (that may or may not be based in reality) and we must find a different lens to view and guide our actions. Once upon a time, most of our decisions were mediated by others. The church or the government told us who to be and how to act. Now people generally bumble around from guru to guru, hoping to find something that will work for them. Unless people have hit rock bottom in their lives, they rarely seek unmediated truth. Often, we humans do what Pilate did. We become overwhelmed by the options ahead of us, throw up our hands, give in to despair, and say, "What is truth?"

Solid Souls Keep The Main Thing

Living true to ourselves and others is brutally difficult, not always because we reject truth but because we get distracted. Life brings constant pressures to move from one thing to another without spending sufficient time to make sure that we are living the lives that we are called to live. I see more souls lost to distraction from the truth than to intentional rejection of truth. As Stephen Covey once said, "the main thing is to keep the main thing the main thing."[6] How do you pay attention to the main thing?

This is part of the training that Reese received as he became an

FBI negotiator. Reese's job in crisis situations was to communicate directly with someone who was making a bad choice. One of those crises involved a mother on the other side of a closed door threatening to kill her children. Attached to that door was a series of explosives designed to blow open the door if it became necessary that the SWAT team enter the room to quickly end the standoff. Reese and another negotiator were positioned between the armed men ready to violently end the situation and the door that was ready to blow. At that moment, his children called to video chat with him to say goodnight, because it was bedtime.

How do you stay focused on what's most important in a moment like this? How could Reese decide between competing demands for his attention? On one hand, a woman was threatening to do horrible things that he could perhaps curtail. On the other hand, he had made a commitment always to speak to his own children before bed every night.

During the coronavirus pandemic, Reese leveraged these kinds of choices to train corporations and others how to thrive, even in the midst of massive stress and competing demands. When Reese trains staff, he has tips and stories to keep focused, such as these:

- *Always remember your primary mission.* My primary mission is to be a good husband / good dad. It doesn't mean that I always drop what I am doing to take a phone call though, because there are times in which I need to focus on what I am doing for my job. But I always make sure that I remember my primary mission.
- *Perspective changes everything.* Different photographs or paintings can be seen from very different perspectives, such as one where you see either a duck or a woman holding a baby. The different perspectives change the reality of the picture for people. For one viewer, the picture portrays

a duck, and this brings up the imagery of water. The another, the picture portrays a woman holding a baby, and this brings up imagery or thoughts of their mom, parents, or grandparents. Both are looking at the exact same thing, but their perceptions are very different. Perspective changes everything. Perhaps the challenges that we face might look different if we saw them through a different lens.

- **Confirmation bias.** Confirmation bias reveals someone's ability or willingness to use context clues around them to support whatever story they have told themselves in their head. Humans are fantastic at spotting patterns. Sometimes, we even spot patterns that do not exist. If you are thinking about yellow cars, you will notice more yellow cars, even if there are the same number of yellow cars that there were previously. The point is that we ought to be suspicious of our own perception.[7]

These tips are small, life strategies to separate out our perceptions from the truth of the world around us. Living true to ourselves requires constant focus on reality and our priorities. When his children called, Reese asked for a "time-out." He was able to take a break and wish his children a good night. This was Reese's value. He felt that his first priority was to be a great father to his little girls and that he could trust the others on his team to do their job while he stepped away. When that was over, he went back in, tapped on the back of his replacement, and re-engaged with the negotiation. The woman and children emerged eventually unharmed, and everyone went home that day.

Reese kept his commitment to his children and to the woman on the other side of the door, because he had a very clear understanding of his values and was able to think clearly enough in order to navigate them that day. Reese knew that God made him to keep the main thing the main thing. Too many souls have let the urgent outweigh the important. If we keep our priorities in order, it is possible to be true to ourselves, our jobs, and our families.

You Control You

A primary rule of negotiation for the FBI is that you never lie. If that happens and you get caught, everything is lost. The difficulty is that we are all in our own pressure-cookers, struggling to figure out how to balance the competing needs of today, and almost none of us have training. To top it all off, every single person we meet brings baggage from their past into every single situation. So how in the world do we have conversations with people that are anywhere near truth?

Truth begins with our souls, being honest with ourselves about who we truly are. Reese's tactics for stress and pressure are mostly ways for us to navigate difficult moments and times in our lives so that we choose not to simply react to the environment around us. If we understand that we are eternal souls and not just reactive animals, then we can take a few moments—even in the midst of high stress and anxiety—to recognize that we get to control how we act in that moment.

During my divorce, I discovered something that should not have been as surprising as it was. I learned that I had no control over other people in my life. I was in a divorce that I did not choose, and yet there was nothing I could do to stop it. In the darkest days of that process, I had only one goal: to be able to look myself in the mirror when I went to bed that night. I knew that I was emotional, fragile, and had somehow failed, and I was not going to use that as an excuse to create more brokenness in my life by making bad decisions. Over time, I came to understand the truth that I could not control someone else. I could only control me.

My job was to be honest with myself. I had to learn what it was about me that encouraged my wife to leave me. This process of self-reflection resulted in "Husband Arthur 2.0," as I described my "new and improved" self in chapter five. I expect that someday I will learn more about myself and become "Husband Arthur 3.0," although this time it will be with the same wife. What I did not know is that my process of self-honesty was not going to end with me simply being a better husband. That process of honesty would one day be necessary in other parts of my life. I showed up at St. Andrew not knowing how to be a good co-worker or a good boss. With blinders of ambition and confidence, I ignored relationships that should have been more like friendships. It would take other moments of self-reflection and brutal honesty to become "Co-worker Arthur 2.0." God willing, that process of honesty, self-reflection, and improvement will continue for the rest of my life.

This is part of what Paul meant when he wrote that we are fighting spiritual battles, not against flesh and blood, but against spiritual forces of wickedness (see Ephesians 6:12). I have known too many pastors who let private sins fester without self-reflection and brutal honesty. If businesses have methods and systems to keep themselves honest so that they do not lose money, why do we not have better systems to keep ourselves honest when the downside is infinitely more than money: we can lose our souls. The first piece of that battle is truth, admitting that we are broken, live in a broken world, and that we must find a better way to live. Like the 12-step programs that address addictions of all kinds, the first step is admitting that we are powerless over our addiction to brokenness.

That truth will set you free.

Vulnerable Love Resonates

In my relationships with my wife, my family, and my co-workers, my key to not repeating my mistakes has been vulnerable love, the kind in which I admit to others what I have learned about myself. Often, I have revealed something that I felt was deep and difficult to share with someone that I love, and that person responded with, "Of course that is true." For example, I am bad at creating systems. I am gifted at strategy and vision but not at creating systems that align large groups of people around that strategy or vision. I thought this was a secret. I did not know that everyone in my workplace knew it but me. I had been told this before by someone who chose to leave our staff. Yet I could not hear it. I finally realized it when we hired someone who was fantastic at creating systems. Only then did I actually understand that I was bad at it. Through a year-long management process, I was blown away to learn about myself what others already knew. There are three crucial learning components to this:

1) **You can't hide.** Adam and Eve tried to hide in the garden, and they failed. The people that love you already know your worst self. Are you a slob? Your spouse knows it. Are you bad at details? Your co-workers know it. Particularly if you are a boss or a parent, someone with authority over other people, those people who are under your authority know that their success and failure is often determined by you. This means they have thought deeply about your quirks and faults. Often they have paid closer attention to your faults and quirks than you.

2) **Your life will be better when you admit the truth.** When I admitted that I was not good at systems, it freed me up to allow others to do that job. When I confessed to staff the things that I was afraid of, it allowed them to support me and care for me. As my wife and I continue to share with each other our most intimate thoughts and feelings, it frees

us from the burden of being alone, and it allows us better to love each other.

3) **Priorities matter.** My first priority is God, being faithful to the one who created me. My second priority is my wife, the partner whom God has given me to walk into the future with hand-in-hand. My third priority is my children whom God has allowed me to lead and shape as they grow up in this world. Only after these relationships are secure is priority given to my role of a pastor and teacher. Living truly ensures that I can be my best self in every one of these relationships, and that requires an honest look at whether I am prioritizing all the things in my life properly.

Vulnerable love is being honest with ourselves and then sharing that honesty with others. Our relationships fail when we refuse to be vulnerable with others. Hiding ourselves from others reduces our relationships from love to transactions. Co-workers who just handle tasks with one another could be satisfied with computers and not souls. Friendships that are only about what one person needs become tedious. Relationships are forged when one person reveals something about himself or herself, and it resonates with the other, and then they share, and it resonates back. This happens because we are honest with ourselves and dare to be honest with someone else.

Seek Truth

As an FBI agent, youth pastor, and accountant, Reese learned the value of taking the time to seek his authentic truth. One of the stories he tells is that, in the middle of a tense trial, he was aware that the terrorists that he had helped to arrest had access to his name. One day, on the way to work—about 25 minutes from his house to his office—a car followed him the entire way. This car made every single turn with him, and Reese became confident that these were bad people following him.

As Reese pulled into the parking lot, he removed the gun from his holster and was about to radio in for backup when the car disappeared. He couldn't find anyone and legitimately thought about sending local police to watch his house. A couple of days went by, and he saw the same car, recognizing the last few digits of the license plate. Reese followed the car into his neighborhood where a garage door went up, dogs came out, and a woman came out and gave the driver a hug and a kiss. His neighbor happened to work next door to him 25 minutes away. Thank goodness Reese discovered the truth. Both people got to go home to their families and live their lives without fear.

The truth will set you free.

PART THREE

Souls Onward And Upward

In 2019, David Brooks, columnist for the *New York Times*, published a book about what he called "the quest for a moral life" in which he introduced a new metaphor for meaning and purpose: "the second mountain." The first mountain of life is one of ambition and striving for achievement. But the top of that mountain is not as satisfying as it appeared from the distance. Brooks writes about his discovery that the true mountain of significance is the second mountain, which is one of purpose, morality, and community. He writes, "If the first mountain is about building up the ego and defining the self, the second mountain is about shedding the ego and losing the self."[1]

This framework reminded me of Jim Collin's definition of the ideal leader. In *Good to Great*, Collins looked at companies that made the transition from good results to excellent results over a sustained period of time. He found that great companies were led by what he called "level 5 leaders." A level 5 leader is a different type of leader than people expect. Level 5 leadership is characterized by "personal humility and indomitable will" for the vision of the organization. In the book, Collins notes that he does not know how to create level 5 leaders, but many had gone through "significant life experiences that might have sparked or furthered their maturation." In other words, they faced a bout of cancer or experienced a loss that gave them a different way to live.[2]

Viewing life with an eternal perspective allows us to become different. It allows us to reach our second mountain or to become people who transform the world from good to great. I do not believe that you have to have gone through divorce, cancer, or loss to achieve this. When golfing as a teenager, I often missed hitting my first ball. Out of frustration, I dropped another ball right there and hit it, simply to prove that I could make the shot. If I was playing with my uncle Randy, he would say, "as the wise man says, hit your second shot first." I did not need to miss my first shot to hit a good shot. I needed to learn how to hit my second shot first. In this last section, we will learn from three people. First, we will learn from Epiphanie, who has experienced the worst that humanity has to offer and proved that the best is still possible. Heaven on earth is possible, and we can make it happen. Next, we will learn from David, who has quit ordained ministry to start numerous businesses. We each have a purpose in life to make a difference in the world. Finally, we will learn from anonymous donors how to leverage everything we have to bring heaven to earth.

I hope that together we can learn how to seek the second mountain first (or second, or third). Wherever you are on your journey, Jesus invites you to start living a life of meaning and purpose. There is never a limit to meaning and purpose. Like Lewis's vision of heaven, the second mountain is one where there is always another level, something new to learn, and someone new to connect with. You may have never organized your life around meaning and purpose. But you can start now. You may be just starting out your life and have come across this book. Listen to the thousands of people who have looked for the first mountain but now seek the one of purpose and meaning. You may have tried to climb the first mountain a hundred times. Start now on your second mountain because it is infinite and eternal. Another level of joy and life is waiting on the second mountain, or as Lewis wrote describing the heavenly journey: onward and upward.[3]

8 | Heaven On Earth Is Possible

The year after I graduated from seminary, I had the privilege of thinking each day about how to transform the lives of African orphans. Zoe Ministry (*Zoe* is the Greek word for "Life") hired me to tell its story of empowering the lives of orphans.[1] Zoe put me in touch with one of the most amazing women that I have ever known, a Rwandan Genocide survivor named Epiphanie Mujawimana. At 9 years old, she was functionally orphaned. Her father had died, and her mother had a disability. Although the world had been cruel, she wasn't without hope. She started a garden, growing onions that she sold on the sides of the road. Epiphanie found a way forward even through grief and difficult times.

When Epiphanie became an adult, the horrors returned as friends and neighbors turned on one another in the ethnic slaughter of Hutus murdering Tutsis. The Rwandan genocide in 1994 was the worst murder of an ethnic group since World War II. The Rwandan dead accumulated at nearly three times the rate of the Jewish dead in the Holocaust.[2] Around one million Tutsis were executed, largely by machete, in about one hundred days. Epiphanie was one of the hunted, barely surviving along with her husband and children.

During the one hundred days, America and other Western countries deliberated and chose not to intervene. While we were legally committed to stopping genocide according to the Geneva Convention, the US government chose to distinguish between "genocide" and "acts of genocide."[3] That legal distinction was a sinful excuse not to involve ourselves. Our inaction was pathetic, and as we saw pictures of the death and destruction, the failure weighed upon our guilt so we sent shipments of supplies and aid to the countless children orphaned by systematic murder.

Epiphanie's job after the genocide was to be one of the people overseeing the distribution of this aid. In her work, she noticed something odd. People had discovered that the bureaucratic nature of distributing aid meant that the less they had, the more they got from America. So they started destroying their possessions. Shouldn't there be a better way? Since she was a little girl, she knew that even those who had been devastated have something to offer the world. How does one person create a better way?

The Whole World Is Asking, Isn't There A Better Way?

Epiphanie's lens as a genocide survivor is unique, but her question is not. In fact, it is a question that is asked every day. Most of us, though, struggle to do anything about it. The world seems structured in a way to encourage a shortened view of life. When Rwandan genocide survivors discover how to get new things by destroying possessions, this isn't the fault of the Rwandans. Rather, it is a consequence of the system. Fortune 500 CEOs and managers make equivalent decisions every day on the publicly-traded stock market.

I have a friend whom we will call Joe. Joe worked for a Fortune 500 company (a publicly traded company that ranks among the largest 500 American corporations by total revenue). The more successful he became in the company, the more he learned how success was rewarded within the organization. Joe's reviews and, therefore, salaries and bonuses were dependent upon his ability to generate quarterly revenues for the company. If you are unfamiliar with corporate structures, here is what you need to know: success is most often defined by stock price. The stock price varies up and down based on a multitude of factors but is significantly affected by the earnings that are required to be reported four times a year. Most public companies hold four calls a year shortly after a quarter is completed.[4] These quarterly reports and earnings calls create massive pressure for the leaders of every publicly traded company.

That pressure is then felt by everyone who works for them. Actions often follow incentives, even if there is a longer vision held by the CEO. If the boss has quarterly pressure, then the people supporting the boss are working with a quarterly lens to their own leadership. The people under them are even further removed from the longer vision and so are looking through only a three-month lens for their work. What happens when someone doing the day-to-day management is trying to look good in this system? They make decisions that are good for the next quarterly earnings report. Sometimes, those decisions are not the best decision for one or two years down the line, but likely those people will be in different jobs—even if in the same company—at which point it will not be their problem.

Not every company has this problem, and many CEOs share a long vision, but the difficulty, as the Rwandan genocide survivors found, is that the structures of our world reward short-term goals. Life, however, is not short-term. A friend of mine was leaving a job and saying goodbye to a co-worker who had worked at the organization for many years. He complimented my friend on having the guts to leave her job and try something new. In response, my friend said reflexively, "I know, life is short, right?" The man responded, "No, you have it wrong. Life is too long to be stuck somewhere." We need a different lens for our work and life because, when we consider that we are eternal souls, the truth is that eternity is too long not to choose joy today.

The difficulty is that through our current lens, we see the way the world moves and assume that it is the only way. Our greatest limit is our belief that there is a limit. Psychologist Benjamin Hardy describes how our environment changes what is possible in every area of our lives. Consider his description of backflips on a motorcycle:

In 2014, Jasyn Roney became the youngest person to successfully land a backflip on a motorcycle. He was only ten years old. But what's even crazier than a ten-year-old doing a backflip on a motorcycle is the fact that backflips were considered impossible, even 'video game material,' back in the late 1980s and early '90s. But to Roney, doing backflips was just something motocross riders did. He grew up in a motocross culture where everyone did backflips. The backflip became a reality back in 1998 when a motocross film spread like wildfire, showing people attempting backflips off a ramp into water. Suddenly, this unbelievable no-one-can-do-that thing became possible.[5]

By 2015, according to Hardy, a cyclist named Josh Sheehan landed the first triple backflip.[6] The backflip hadn't been possible because people did not believe it was possible. The environment of their culture and brains informed them of a new reality, and suddenly people could do it. The same was true of running a four-minute mile. It was believed to be impossible, but one person did it, and it took only two months for the next person to do it. Now, over a thousand people have done what was once deemed impossible.[7]

We go to work and engage in the culture of our workplace assuming that our current reality is all that is possible. This cannot be true. There must be better ways. Can our companies care for profits *and* their communities? Can our charitable giving stop incentivizing people to remain destitute? My friend Joe chose to leave his company and decided to work for an organization structured around long-term vision rather than quarterly earnings. He understood that there are other choices to make in our lives, in which we are not dependent upon the incentives of the rest of the world. Joe believes in an eternal lens, one that opens up our ability to see possibilities. My friend Epiphanie did the same.

Zoe's Empowerment Program

The standard model of orphan engagement is orphanages. For a child who is able to find a spot, an orphanage or a home can be a fantastic and life-changing thing, but after the Rwandan Genocide and the later HIV/AIDS pandemic, there were too many orphans. In a small region in Kenya where Zoe Ministries ministered during my time in the organization (2009–2010), there were an estimated 300,000 orphans. You would have needed 1,000 orphanages, each holding 300 children, to accommodate that one need, and this was only one tiny region of Kenya. There had to be another way. Epiphanie looked around at her country and realized that she could not create a building large enough for the children who needed support and transformation.

The key factor of Zoe's empowerment program is the fundamental belief that children are not helpless.[8] Remembering her little onion garden that generated income after her father died, Epiphanie began to gather young children and teach them tools and tricks to look after themselves. Over time, with a little trial and error, she created and replicated a model and system of orphan empowerment that lasted two to three years. By the end of that three-year process, the orphans no longer needed help. They would have a community to support them, roofs over their head, food to eat, and a way to make money.

The secret, she said, was giving them less.

How in the world is giving an orphan less the best way? She said, "What the children need is the dignity to be able to help themselves. When you hand someone something you have changed that relationship. When you help them help themselves, then they get to the point where they no longer need you."[9]

The program, which boasts over 124,000 alumni and 58,400 children in seven countries,[10] has seen children leverage their infinite creativity and live different lives. I don't know that I would have believed the claims had I not been there myself to see it. These children have grown their own food, started small businesses, and learned about health and hygiene, all in a small community of people that supports one another. One child would learn to sew and create a sewing business. Another had a large plot of land, and the others would help him or her farm and till it, buying animals and creating a working farm. One of my favorites was a boy named Dickens who created a business in which he hired other children. They were breaking apart rocks for use in construction. This boy had gone from being a destitute orphan living on scraps to running a legitimate construction company with dozens of employees. The stories go on and on and on.

Epiphanie knew these children were neither worthless nor helpless. They had unbelievable gifts with infinite possibilities in front of them. Most people would have asked the question, what can I do for these orphans? But Epiphanie taught that this is the wrong question to ask. If we start with the assumption that we are all eternal beings, it becomes possible to ask a different question. What if there is a better way? Epiphanie learned to ask, what can these orphans do for themselves?

Heaven Is As Possible As Hell On Earth

One of the favorite phrases that we use at my church is that there is a "thin veil" between heaven and earth and that there are moments where there is a tear between the two. It is as if we see what our world could be. There are big and small moments where this happens, like the birth of a child or a particularly fragrant summer night after a rain. But these moments are few and far between. My hope is to help us see through that veil more clearly and, at times, remove it altogether to see that heaven is possible on earth.

We do not have to convince ourselves that hell is possible on earth, especially when we have just been introduced to Epiphanie, a survivor of genocide by machete. The world seems to be headed toward hell. Grief, pain, greed, selfishness, and isolation are easy to find, expected even. We are waiting to find holes in the best of us. When everything is good and right in the world and it seems as if heaven is winning, we are still skeptical, waiting for the inevitable flaws. We aren't skeptical when we hear the worst about people; rather, we nod our heads, because our fundamental belief in the darkness of our world has been confirmed yet one more time.

If hell is downstream, why not join it? Because it is not inevitable. We have a choice (or not) to choose what everyone else is doing. We also have a choice to see the world differently and choose something different. Heaven is possible in our lives and in the institutions, systems, and structures of the world.

Often, we Christians get caught up in the question of free will versus determinism. Do we actually have a choice? Benjamin Hardy addresses this question from a non-religious perspective, here quoting Harvard psychologist Ellen Langer: "the more mindful we are, the more we can create the contexts we are in . . . and believe in the possibility of change." Hardy continues with his own commentary: "Thus, it's not free will *or* determinism. It's not choice *or* environments. Instead, it is choice *and* environment. More directly, it is the choice *of* environment. You are responsible for shaping and choosing the environments that will ultimately shape the person you become and the destiny you have."[11] We get to choose the trajectory that we are on. That begins with choosing an environment in which we can believe that heaven is actually possible here on earth.

Zoe's empowerment program works because it inspires children to imagine a different world. Through small working groups that meet weekly, the children begin to form a different vision, not one of begging and humiliation, but one of entrepreneurship and hope. They believe that heaven is possible on earth. Groups based on 12-step programs likewise are full of people who have gone through hell on earth and have chosen a different trajectory. What they are doing is choosing to create and live in an environment in which hell is not inevitable. Heaven is here, right now, available for the taking.

If you find that difficult to believe, then you may need to look at the environment in which you find yourself. Have you been to church recently? Have you read the Scriptures? Prayed? We are so deeply shaped by our community and environment that sometimes we have come to believe that heaven is not possible simply because no one else around us believes that heaven is possible. Change that. Find at least one person—a friend or a spouse—with whom you can whisper about your hopes and dreams. When you have moments where the thin veil between heaven and earth are torn down, share those moments, and see who shares those feelings with you.

As in a backflip on a motorcycle or running a four-minute mile, begin to believe that the impossible is true. If you don't have faith that it is possible, then for a moment borrow my belief that it is. I believe that it is possible because you are, like my friends in Africa, of infinite worth and value. I have faith in heaven on earth because I have seen an orphan move from despair to dignity. I have seen businesses transform entire communities. I have seen heaven here on earth, and it is far more fulfilling and amazing than the petty isolation of hell.

We Can Swim Upstream

We are infinite souls on a path toward heaven or hell, but that doesn't mean that we are all perfect saints or all broken sinners. Each of us have moments in which we choose heaven or hell. We are both saints and sinners. Our lives and souls are rarely that simple. In fact, we all have moments where we go up or down:

Consider me. I am a fifth-generation Methodist preacher. My calling to ministry came before elementary school, and I have been on this path my entire life. I spend my life telling people that heaven is possible here on earth, but those who know me best know that I do not always choose heaven. There are times when I choose what is wrong for me and my family. That level of nuance is often difficult for people to understand. People tend to put preachers or leaders on a pedestal and imagine that their lives are perfect. One person has even said to my wife in a wistful voice, "It must be great to be married to Arthur," as if she assumed that I never got angry or was selfish. Becky responded that it is great, but it is not perfect. In fact, if there is anything Becky wants people to know, it is that we also have our struggles and difficulties.

Every single one of the saints that we put on pedestals are broken people. It doesn't help me, Epiphanie, or any Christian leader to be seen in such a way. In the end, we will choose either heaven or hell, but every human whom you have ever met is trying to navigate those choices at almost every moment. The inverse is also true. Every person whom we believe is too broken to be redeemed is also someone who has the potential to make more heavenly choices.

The paths of our lives are never simple and clean, but they do trend one way or the other. The secret to choosing heaven is to never to stop seeking the better way. We are not perfect, but we can keep working toward perfection. We fail when we assume that the world is simply what it is and that no one can change it. That can't be true because there are people who have changed the world. If one person has changed the world, then it means that anyone can change the world. It means that you can change the world.

Change is hard and slow at first, because change is exponential. Transformation compounds over time. But change is possible.

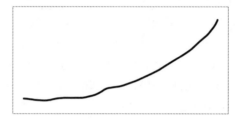

If you look at this graph and view only the first few steps, it looks like nothing is really happening. We often give up because those first few steps are so difficult. Other people likely won't appreciate the steps you are taking. Sometimes they will try to sabotage those steps. Living as if there is a better way sometimes feels like judgment to those who have already given up and are simply riding the path downstream. In the moments where we stumble and fall, others will laugh and find it as proof that swimming upstream is not actually possible. There are those who are hoping we fail as proof that we should never have tried. But that is because they don't yet see a different trajectory as possible in their own lives.

But if we keep seeking perfection, then our lives will look more like this:

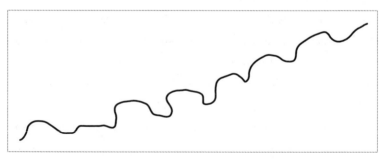

If you look at any one moment, it feels random. But if we always think there is a better way, then, even through the ups and downs of life, we can create an exponential curve of heaven that expands and compounds.

There is a better way. It just isn't a straight line. It is waking up every day believing that there is a better way. When we fail (*when*, not *if*), we get up the next day and choose again. Heaven is possible, or as Jesus said in his first sermon, "The kingdom of God has come near. Repent and believe the good news" (Mark 1:15). Choose your trajectory carefully.

Orphans Adopting Orphans

Epiphanie's first groups were difficult. She needed time to figure out a system that worked and a way of assisting the orphans without crippling them. She needed them to foster their own sense of worth and competence. Over time, one group became two. Two became four and eventually grew to more than 124,000 orphans. In my ten years connected to this ministry, I have seen ups and downs, but the consistent belief that heaven is possible has continued to provoke expansion, even in ways that we could not have imagined.

One of my favorite realizations about Zoe and this amazing ministry is that the impact is far larger than we originally intended. Heaven is not only possible; it also expands. What Epiphanie did not expect was that the orphans would themselves help other orphans. One young man I met in rural Kenya was named Davis. As a teenager, Davis had lost both parents and was caring for his younger siblings. As orphans, he and his best friend Sqberio had worked together to survive. As Zoe moved into their neighborhood, Davis was enrolled in Zoe's empowerment program. He learned that he had infinite worth and value and started a business with his group called the Blessings Bakery. Each of the orphans in the group sold the bread made by Davis, and he earned three dollars a day. For the first time, he was earning money. He even started a bank account to save the money.

But he wasn't satisfied because he knew that his friend Sqberio was still hungry. So Davis gave him a job. He split his daily income in half ($1.50 each) between the two of them as they baked bread together. Over time, he walked Sqberio into a bank to open his own bank account. When I met them, they had started to make more money. They were proud of their accomplishments. They did not see themselves as victims with no way out but as friends of infinite worth who have the means to transform their lives and the lives of their families.

Epiphanie knew that children had value and could make money, but even she did not fully grasp the infinite possibilities when people learn to swim upstream. This is what happens when people believe that heaven is possible. They start imagining a whole new world, a world that could become even better than they could possibly imagine. If it is true for an orphan, it is true for you and for me, and that journey is possible because of our belief in the Christian story and that every single person is a child of God.

Reegan Kaberia, the chief program officer of Zoe, says that every empowerment program begins with a gathering of the orphans. While Zoe is explicitly Christian in framework and belief, the children are not necessarily Christian and are not forced to become so in the process; all children are welcome in the program. At the first meeting with the orphans, he begins with the Lord's Prayer, which begins, "Our father who art in heaven." He stops and says to the children, "You see! You are not orphans. You have a father who made you and loves you. There is no need for shame because you are loved." He told me that the belief in God, or at least the belief that Reegan believes in God, can change their lives. Many children have entered the room with their heads down, not believing that they are of value, and have left with their heads held up high, having learned they have worth.

A belief that heaven is possible here on earth takes away the limitations of the world. People believe that the world cannot change, and so it doesn't. People believe that they cannot change, and so they don't. People believe that the systems and companies of our world cannot change, and so they do not try.

The children at Zoe are told that they are made in the image of God and that they have a God who loves them. Is it any wonder that they adopt other orphans? They have seen themselves and their situation change, and so they spread the good news. Good news, of course, is what Jesus was all about when he began his ministry, telling everyone that he could meet, "The kingdom of heaven is near!" In case you do not know, "good news" is the English translation of the Greek word *gospel* in the scriptures.

I have been changed and have written this book in part because I befriended orphans who adopted other orphans because of their belief in a heavenly father. Once I saw the good news of heaven on earth, anything less became unacceptable.

9 | What Were You Made To Do?

You are an eternal soul created on purpose, but to do what exactly? In God's desire to create a better world, and for our souls to be more solid, how do we know what we are supposed to be doing?

This is the question that nagged my friend David Michel. David was smart, capable, and believed in God, but exactly what was he supposed to do? He started off majoring in business, took an economics course and hated it. So he switched to mechanical engineering and took classes in statistics, dynamics, and thermodynamics. He did well in those, but he knew it wasn't for him, so he switched his major to geology. He chose that because he went to a counselor and said, "I just want to graduate in time. What can I do after all of these classes that will allow me to do that?" He ended up with a major in chemistry and a minor in geology.[1]

A year after he graduated, David went to seminary at Perkins School of Theology at Southern Methodist University to become an ordained minister in The United Methodist Church. He wanted to see whether he was called by God to be a pastor. In high school and again in college, David had experienced a life-changing community where he had encountered a living God. His grandmother was so thrilled that he was becoming a pastor, she said, "Oh Dave, I can die now. I have a grandson who is going to be a preacher!"

While David knew that faith mattered, and he enjoyed his classes, he always felt like something was not quite right. He was never quite sure that he was doing exactly what God had called him to do. At the time, Perkins's learning model had students spend two years in classes, one year as a local church intern, then a final year back in the classroom. His internship was at St. Andrew, the church where, twenty-five years later, I would be appointed as an associate pastor as my first full-time church job. He loved it. His job was evangelism—the church was newly started at that time—and he spent three nights a week visiting different families who had attended the church. He got to know the church, played golf with new church members, and he had a blast. The question for David was, what if he liked ministry just because he liked that one job at that one church? Surely liking the people and having fun wasn't the goal, right?

David then asked to serve as a pastor somewhere else, to see if he truly liked being a people's pastor. He was sent to be the pastor of two small churches outside of Denton, Texas. These churches offered nothing like the excitement of the new church start of St. Andrew. The house that the church provided for him and his wife had a carpet filled with fleas and was such a disappointment that the mover pulled up to the house, looked him in the eye, and asked, "Are you sure about this?"

David was sure that he had to try. His first Sunday, he had a fight with a long-time member about whether the curtains covering the side windows would remain closed or not. Once that church member left in protest, the church began to grow. When he got there, as he described it, the church had fourteen to seventeen "gray heads" and no kids. The Sunday after the church member left in protest, eighty people showed up, including families and children. The church thrived.

The problem was that, while the church thrived, David didn't. He was effective but not called. "I learned that, for me, my calling was not to ordained ministry and all that it means," said David, "The seven-day cycle and preaching every Sunday wasn't for me." He then had to call his boss, his bishop, and his grandmother and tell them that this path wasn't right. "[My grandmother] loved me," he said, "but she never really understood why I got out."

What Are You Called To Do Today?

Everyone is called to do something on this earth. I knew that I was called to be a pastor before I started elementary school. One reason that I like David's story is that it is so different from my own. Where I was confident about my path, David was unsure about his. My first sermon was in the sixth grade at First United Methodist Church in Commerce, Texas. I went straight from high school to college and from college to seminary. I have felt called by God to be a pastor almost my entire life.

Friends have told me that this is the most unrelatable part of my life. Most people do not have a set calling that they understand for their lives. I have counseled a lot of people through this fundamental question: "What am I supposed to do?" But I never felt like I had a good answer because I saw it through my own lens. I felt called to only one thing, so I assumed that they would be called to only one thing, but this is not how life works for everyone.

St. Andrew has a credentialed nurse on staff who teaches theology to eighth and ninth graders. A man in my small group, who has a degree in Health Care Administration, now works on business deals related to intellectual property. My wife has a graduate degree in Higher Education Administration and, for at least this time when our children are young, she feels called to stay at home and invest in them. Who knows what tomorrow holds for any of us!

The future is not written. There is a God who is working to bring about heaven on earth right now, and God wants us involved in that. For some like me, there will be one major calling in their lives that will stand out for them. Someone who felt called to medical school and became a doctor may be a practicing doctor for the rest of his or her working life. But that is not the totality of who that person is. Sometimes that person may also be called to lead mission trips during their vacation time every year, or to teach Sunday school for third graders.

One of the things that God has been teaching me over the last ten years is that, while I am called to lead a church for the rest of my working years, that isn't everything that I am called to do. I am called to be a great husband to Becky and a great dad to Sam and Ella Reece. I am gifted in creative thinking and problem solving and love helping my friends in their businesses. I am not limited by my calling but am continually empowered to use the set of gifts given to me by God. God is always calling me to engage the world with those gifts.

In 2019, I was asked to speak at a local high school baccalaureate, which is a semi-religious graduation experience. I was asked to talk about God and the students's future and to bring to them a message about what was possible. My message to them asserted that they had been asked the wrong questions for the last few years, and they would continue to be asked the wrong questions for the next few years. High school students are often asked *where* they are going and *what* they are going to do next. They had been asked *where* they were planning to attend college, if any. They were asked *what* they would major in or *what* job they wanted to do. I think that these are the least interesting set of questions they could have been asked.

Does it really matter if someone goes to Kansas University or Missouri University? Texas A&M or the University of Texas? Or if someone chooses a trade school or to jumps straight into work? Perhaps you know people who have done each of these things and found an amazing life! The most interesting question is not *what* people want to do or *where* they are going to do it, but rather, *who* are they called to be? It matters much more how high schoolers treat the people around them and whether they are doing whatever they are called to do to the best of their ability.

Each person is made by God and is uniquely gifted. God is calling every person to do something unbelievable. This is what David discovered. Discovering your calling is for more than just ministers. In figuring out his future, David consulted with the pastor of Highland Park United Methodist Church, which sits right next to SMU's campus. He had a conversation about his future. He said he felt called to ministry, but now he was feeling that it wasn't quite right. The pastor said to him: "You followed your call right through these doors, and you need to follow this call right out. Just because you aren't called to ordained ministry doesn't mean you aren't called for ministry. I happen to think that the opportunity for ministry is greater on the other side of the pulpit than they are for me."

Everyone is called to bring heaven to earth. You are called to bring heaven to earth. How? By being the most faithful version of yourself, even if that means making a change.

Authentically David

Once David made the call to leave full-time local church ministry, he had to figure out a whole new path in life. He had a degree in chemistry, a master's in theology, one year of working in admissions at SMU, and his experience as a local church pastor. What job should he apply for? He chose sales, figuring that, in leading a growing church, he had been in sales of a sort. He worked very successfully doing sales for a couple of years, becoming the top seller at his company, then quit that job.

Sales was the second successful career that David had given up. He had proven his ability to lead a growing church and to be a successful salesperson. But neither of them felt right, and David had a unique clarity. He knew that it had to be right. He said, "I think the most fundamental calling that all of us has is to be authentic to who God created us to be. We have to discover who we are created to be and have to be authentic."

Later in his life, with the assistance of a leadership program, David wrote a purpose statement, which said, "My purpose is to lead and create for the greater good." Church ministry didn't fit for him. He needed more innovation and activity. Neither did sales; it had to be for the greater good.

He decided to start a children's television show. He called it *Jay Jay the Jet Plane*. In 1994, with no experience in television, animation, or storytelling, David quit a successful sales job to lead a new team and create something new for the greater good. That year, *Power Rangers* had been a popular children's TV show, and David thought there ought to be positive, nonviolent, wholesome role models for young children. He found script writers, modelers, animators, and—although it was difficult and very close to failing a number of times—it worked. More important, it was a calling: "At a time in the early 2000s, we had over a million kids in the US watching every day. In the church, I would have had the opportunity to impact whoever came on Sunday. On PBS, I had a million kids watching. For me, that was impact." The series would end up with forty-five episodes and stay on the PBS Kids network through reruns until 2009.

It is important to note that David had been successful in all three areas. The question wasn't what could he do, but rather, what should he do? What would give him energy and excitement to get up in the morning? Although his grandmother never fully understood his leaving ministry, David knew that it had to be right. "I know so many pastors who at some point or another knew it wasn't quite right, but they stayed with it," said David. "It was the safer and easier path, but those folks aren't very happy right now. They aren't in the right place for them." David could not deny being who God authentically made him to be.

David continued to start new companies which allowed him to lead and create for the greater good. After he launched *Jay Jay*, David started another company called *Winning Habits* which helped people identify bad habits and replace them with winning habits. He sold that company. He then bought a piece of another company called *Inner Change* and ran it for four years. It operated treatment centers for teen girls and young women who have gotten way off track with eating disorders, drug addictions, depression, self-harm, and other issues. After he sold that company, he started his latest project in 2011 called *Catapult Health* whose mission is to help people make great improvement for themselves.

What do these companies have in common? Only one thing that mattered: they let David be authentically David. They allowed him to lead and create for the greater good: "We know when we are being authentic to who God created us to be. We just have to discover what it is. Once we discover what it is, we can't deny it."

David could not deny the calling God had on his life—and it has impacted millions of people.

Souls On Fire

How about you? Who were you made to be? What are your gifts? Try not to think about categories of education or careers like doctor or lawyer. Look deeper at the core combination of attributes and desires that make your soul crackle like a fire. Civil rights leader and pastor Howard Thurman says it this way, "Don't ask what the world needs. Ask yourself what makes you come alive and then go do that. Because what the world needs is people who have come alive."[2] God wants this world to be better than it is. Heaven on earth is the goal! Why would we limit ourselves to the categories that already exist when we are confident that there is a better way, and that God wants us to participate in that better way? Rather, ask yourself what makes you excited to wake up in the morning. What sets your soul on fire?

How can you know what you were made to do? There are countless ways to find out. I will give a few examples of how it has worked for me and how I have seen it work for others:

- *Understand the stories of your past.* My wife had the privilege of going through a process at "The Giftedness Center" with Bill Hendricks in Dallas. He had her write down all the times in her life when something worked for her in a unique way that made her happy. They sat down and talked about her life, and he explored what it was about each of those moments that made her feel alive, that set her soul on fire. He outlines this process in *The Person Called You: Why You're Here, Why You Matter & What You Should Do with Your Life.*[3] Years after she sat down with Bill, we have gone back to the core insights that he gleaned from her past. Your own past is holding clues to who God has made you to be. There have been times in your life when your soul was on fire. When were those times? When were you the most solid version of yourself

- *Ask other people about your gifts.* Lots of people have ideas for your life, including parents, grandparents, children, friends, and even people you do not know well. David's grandmother wanted the best for him but was stuck on a certain job and not the core question about David's gifts and where he could be most authentically David. Talk to all sorts of people, not about what they think you ought to do, but rather ask them, when do they like being around you the most? Experiencing people as their best authentic selves is an exciting thing. Ask your parents, friends, children, and co-workers when they have seen you most fulfilled.

• *Focus on your strengths.* Twenty years ago, the Gallup organization created the "StrengthsFinder Test" (now the "Clifton Strengths Assessment") after interviewing more than 1.7 million professions.[4] Millions of people have taken this exam. The test lists thirty-four categories of strengths, which we can call talents or gifts. The test identifies the top five strengths of each person. David's strengths revealed his characteristics as Activator, Maximizer, Woo, Communication, and Futuristic. My strengths are in Strategic, Ideation, Belief, Woo, and Communication. David and I have two of our five top strengths in common, but his match—who God has made him to be—and my match—who God has made me to be—are different. The point of the StrengthsFinder is to focus on "what is 'right' about people, not 'wrong' with them." Every single person has gifts and strengths. focusing on what you are naturally good at is a way to understand how you were made.

• *Ask God.* You are not alone in figuring out who you are supposed to be. This is why I use the phrase "your calling." There is a God who is actively working with you to bring you to a place where you are on fire and the world is transformed. When you pray, don't just ask for the easiest path or the way that causes the least difficulty. Pray for what God wants, because what God wants is for you to be on fire and the world transformed. Jesus told his disciples to pray like this:

> "Our Father in heaven, hallowed be your name,
> your kingdom come, your will be done,
> on earth as it is in heaven" (Matthew 6:9-10).

This concept—God's will being done on earth as it is in heaven—is asking for heaven to come to earth. What you may not know is that, when you pray, God wants to engage with you to transform this world into exactly that. Prayer is asking God to use you to bring heaven to earth. Just ask God to change you and use you for Jesus's mission and glory. God will do the rest.

Your Highest Self

You were made on purpose for a purpose. You are not an accident. You are a gift to this world, and your strengths and gifts are needed. God wants you to become your fullest self. Often, the difference between a solid and a shriveled soul is whether our gifts make us better or we use them as an excuse. God did not make us unique so that we can justify bad behavior, like the internet meme falsely attributed to Marilyn Monroe, "If you can't handle me at my worst, you don't deserve me at my best." Rather, our gifts ought to make us better people to be around at all times. In the second section of this book, I described how souls are meant to be in community with one another. Being gifted at our work and in our jobs is not an excuse for neglecting the other parts of our lives. Instead, our gifts ought to enhance the other parts of our lives. My wife loves that I love my job and that I continue to be excited every week that I get to go to church and lead people. At its best, the work that I do makes me happier when I come home and engage with my family. My best self is to be a great pastor/preacher and a great husband/father/friend.

Keep asking yourself: Is what I am doing making me a fuller version of myself or a shriveled, less authentic version of myself? It is a balance that we navigate every day. In my job, there is always work to be done, sermons and books to write, and conversations to have with church members or prospective church members. How do I navigate this? By being clear about what makes me the best version of me, and by deliberately choosing to spend my time focused on my purpose and aligned with my values.

This is how that works its way out in my life: My purpose is to "Enthusiastically lead people to a new trajectory of a solid earthly and eternal life." David and I went through the same program, and I too worked hard on being clear about what I am called to do here on earth. The word *enthusiasm* is critical. If you ask people I work with what is best about working with me, most of them would say it is when I get excited about what we are doing. Others get excited around me in those times. I know that my role is to lead. I love the task and privilege of leading a group of people as a pastor every week. The word *trajectory* is a common one for me in my preaching and in this book. Everyone has the chance to live a new trajectory that points toward their highest self. My job is to help people see that they can have a solid earthly and eternal life. Heaven is here now. You reading this book is part of me living out my purpose on earth. I believe that you can lead a completely new life, that you have a unique purpose, and you're your purpose is best lived out with clear values.

I know that my values include the following:

- **Faith.** I spend time with God through personal prayer, family prayers, and reading of Scripture.
- **Tribal Fulfillment.** I prioritize time with my wife and children, our extended family, and a handful of close friends, such as our small group. I make sure there is time for this small group of people we call our "tribe."
- **Mature Integrity.** I minimize drama and gossip, am faithful to God, my wife, my calling, and my church.
- **Impact.** I engage with organizations and people to make a difference, to make sure that I am on a new and better

trajectory in every place that I spend time. I am not here simply to keep things the way they are but to make an impact for a better world.

- **A Good Life.** I make life fun with date time with my wife, golf with friends, and play time with my kids. I have a *banquet* mindset where I revel in moments of joy and celebration.

These are my values. In our family retreat every year, I revisit these values, and I ask my wife if I am living up to them. I have shared them with a friend and co-worker at church, who also regularly challenges me if I am not living up to my goals and values.

One difficulty in our world is that we talk about ourselves as if we were fixed, saying to the world, "This is who I am; deal with it." That isn't how souls work. Of course, you are you, but you can become more solid or more shriveled. You can be preoccupied with tiny and inconsequential things, or you can be fully you. Spend time thinking through your purpose. What were you made to do? Spend time thinking about your values. If you are living your most solid life, what do you prioritize?

Our Futures

Our futures are not set. I have no idea what David is going to do with the next part of his life, and neither does he! I am confident that he will continue to lead and create for the common good. During the COVID pandemic, the business model at *Catapult Health*, where David worked, broke. The way they "help people make great improvement for themselves" was to do yearly health checkups at workplaces to make it more likely that people would take the time to do a yearly blood and health screening. When businesses shut down in March 2020, their revenue plunged. What did David do?

Fortunately, David was clear in his purpose. He led and created for the common good. In just four months, he led his team to re-think their entire business model, and they created a new product: the virtual checkup. They deliver a box in the mail to a patient with a free measuring tape for your waist, a free blood-pressure monitor, and a set of instructions. The patient mails back a sample of blood from a pin prick, and then speaks with a nurse practitioner about his or her health and future. Patients don't have to go to an office and wait in line. They get to improve their lives without leaving the house. This past October, the company reached its best month in its history, and people find it easier to make their lives better. This is the kind of creative thinking that God has in mind for us.

God has given each of us gifts and is calling each of us to engage in the world to make it more like heaven on earth. God wants you to be a part of it. What are you called to do in the world? What sets your soul on fire and makes you the best version of yourself?

Do it today. The world needs you. God needs you.

10 | Leave It All Out On The Field

What are you going to do when you no longer need what you have?

Like a coach reminding his players before the final game, there is a time limit that we each have on earth. Done right, that time is glorious. Vince Lombardi, famous coach of the Green Bay Packers, said, "I firmly believe that any man's finest hour, the greatest fulfillment of all that he holds dear, is that moment when he has worked his heart out in a good cause and lies exhausted on the field of battle, victorious."[1] As every good coach knows, the worst feeling after a game is to think that you could have done something more.

Since our souls do not die with our bodies, the same is true for the whole of life. I learned this lesson from a family who prefers to remain anonymous, but we will call them the "Spark Tank" family.

A little over six years ago, a couple invited my wife and me out to dinner. We had been to dinner with this family before, so this wasn't unusual, except that we were told that they had an idea to talk to us about. After we sat down and had appetizers, they handed over a piece of paper that had the rough outline of a goal. They wanted to give $500,000, over three years, to the church to inspire people to engage with the world differently. We had been in the middle of a sermon series talking about the kingdom of heaven; if we could only see the world the way God does, we could experience heaven on earth. They had looked at their financial goals and decided that, if they believed that this was true, they ought to put their money to work. Lots of people give money to the church, but often it is for the annual operating budget or buildings. This couple had one goal: to give away their money in such a way that people would see that all that we have on earth is meant to be used to bring about a better world.

We talked for hours about ways to do this. Someone mentioned the idea of giving away cash to people at church and telling them to hand that cash to the next person they see (outside of church, of course) and tell them that God loves them. It seemed problematic to hand out $166,667 in cash on a single weekend, although it would have accomplished the goal, which was not simply to do the most good but to get the most people to realize that they can bring heaven to earth. We decided to imagine it as a matching-funds challenge program in which the church would reimburse 50 percent of anything people would do that was good in the world. This became known as the "Spark Tank."

Over three summers, we witnessed more than three hundred fifty projects generate more than $800,000 worth of impact in the community. More important, the Spark Tank family gave me and a few thousand other people at the church the opportunity to re-imagine what our impact on the world should be. Every weekend for three straight summers, I got to look at our church and say that a family gave half a million dollars to challenge them to do something—anything—to bring the kingdom of heaven to earth. It made our church think about our own resources. Did we have the guts and confidence to do what the "Spark Tank" family did?

Irrelevant Faith

On a summer day almost three hundred years ago, a preacher named John Wesley stepped into the pulpit at St. Mary's in Oxford and preached a sermon about actual versus knock-off faith. This was a more exhilarating sermon than it might sound, because Wesley accused the people in the pews listening that day—the educated religious academics of Oxford University—of not actually being Christians. The sermon, "The Almost Christian," targeted those who lived a semi-spiritual life with the "form of godliness" but without the actual love of God and love of neighbor that Jesus demands.

Sermons like this made Wesley an enemy to the "established religion" of the Church of England. He was frequently barred from preaching inside churches and resorted to preaching outside to large crowds of people, who were amazed to hear the gospel preached as if it mattered to their lives. Famously, he was once even barred from the church where his father was buried. So he stood on his father's tomb to preach the message that God wants them to become "altogether Christians," or people who live their entire lives for God. This was a peculiar message for a population where, functionally, everyone was Christian. Christianity was the religion of the country, but few people went to church. Wesley took the religious leaders of the day to task.

Standing in their pulpits, Wesley provoked people by asking:

> Are not many of you conscious, that you never came thus far; that you have not been even almost a Christian. . . . You never so much as intended to devote all your words and works, your business, studies, diversions, to his glory. You never even designed or desired, that whatsoever you did should be done "in the name of the Lord Jesus, and as such should be "a spiritual sacrifice, acceptable to God through Christ.[2]

No wonder he was rejected by the church: he accused them of lying about their faith! When people see the church and its leaders not living the faith they claim to profess, why would anyone think that faith could make a difference? Faith becomes culturally irrelevant. In the eighteenth century, the church was an established political structure, not a place to have your heart set on fire. Are we that much different today?

Wesley's solution was to lead a group of people who would be methodical about their search to have their faith make a difference in their lives. They would be defined by asking a crucial question every day: "How is it with your soul?"[3]

Wesley did not think he was doing anything new. In fact, he kept saying that he was trying to restore Christianity to its original power. He wanted to gather a people who fully loved God: "Such a love is this, as engrosses the whole heart, as rakes up all the affections, as fills the entire capacity of the soul and employs the utmost extent of all its faculties."[4] And a people that fully loved their neighbor: "And is this commandment written in your heart, 'That he who loveth God love his brother also.' Do you then love your neighbor as yourself? Do you love every man, even your enemies, even the enemies of God, as your own soul as Christ loved you?"[5]

Faith is irrelevant and dull when it is done in part and only when convenient. There is another way; live our lives fully to God and be faithful even when inconvenient.

Exhilarating Faith

The "Spark Tank" project was fun. For three summers, St. Andrew families dreamed about how they could live to make a difference. What was particularly amazing was that, when you set the vision for bringing heaven to earth—sparking a difference in the world, people came up with projects and ministries that were beyond any one person's imagination.

One group held a "Spark Tank" party where they decided to pay for people's meals at a drive-through restaurant. The group went to a local hamburger chain restaurant and paid for a couple of hundred dollars's worth of meals. The goal was to help them express that we were doing this because God loves them, and that is simply what people who love God do. One guy in the group named Joe asked whether he could get in the window and tell people why we were paying for their meal. He put on the company's hat, used a "Spark Tank" gift card where he had paid for half and the "Spark Tank" family paid for the other half, and he talked to the people coming through the drive-through, telling them that this was a project of the church.

This was not a boring moment. Faith wasn't irrelevant; it was exhilarating. The burger restaurant staff had never had anyone do this before. The people in line were expecting to pay for their food and instead met someone, who clearly didn't work at the restaurant, who joked with them and told them that their food was paid for by the church. The group gathered afterward and laughed about Joe in the burger hat for hours. This wasn't awkward evangelism where we walk up to strangers talking about faith. Instead, we lived it and demonstrated that what we believe about God and our neighbor is real and is a blast to live out.

Another project came up when a church member, Christine, read the local Dallas newspaper. She found an article that described Dallas families who were being forced to choose between feeding their families and doing laundry.[6] The article told of an effort by Tom Hayden, who oversees volunteer and partnership services for the Dallas Independent School District, to buy washers and dryers for public schools. Children who could not come to school in clean clothes often would not come at all, and Tom thought that there was a way to fix that. Christine immediately thought of the "Spark Tank" and went to her connection group. The group was excited about doing the project. They raised $5,000, which was matched by $5,000 from the "Spark Tank" family. The $10,000 not only paid for ten washers and dryers for local schools but also the permit and plumbing work that needed to be done. A small group at one local church paid for new plumbing at a Dallas elementary that had been built in the 1930s. Christine wrote an email to Hayden and immediately got a response that said, "God answers prayers."

According to Tonya Clark, the principal, the attendance rate in the school after the installation of the washers and dryers went up to close to the national average. Tom Hayden remarked that the happiness in the hallways was noticeably up after the installation. It makes sense that children who are not ashamed of the cleanliness of their clothes are both happier and more willing to come to school. The students were happier, but so were the church members. They got the opportunity to see a need in their community and make a difference.

The advantage of the "Spark Tank" project is that people had an existing structure to give them the spark to do something about the problems that they saw. How many church-going Christians in the Dallas-Fort Worth region saw that article about Tom's project? How many times have we walked by a fast-food restaurant or gotten groceries and not thought about the opportunities to make a difference in that moment? What the "Spark Tank" family knew is that every moment can yield new opportunities to make people's faith real in their lives. In a video to our church, expressing what she wanted to convey to her fellow church members, one member of the group said, "When you finally get your eyes opened to what opportunities are out there, [the possibilities are] endless."[7]

True faith is not irrelevant; it's exhilarating. True faith makes our souls alive and full of joy. These stories about life transformation are not just about doing good deeds in our own lives but about souls flourishing in such a way that they inspire and impact other souls around them.

Accounting In Heaven

Jesus spoke often about scenarios in which we account for our actions on earth when we arrive in heaven. Jesus asked people to repent and have faith but also that faith is supposed to do something. Below are two parables that Jesus tells about accounting for our resources here on earth. If you have read or heard these parables before, take the time to read them again, slowly. Jesus tells these parables so that we might imagine that we are the characters in the story.

Parable of the Faithful and Wise Servant
Matthew 24:45-51

"Who then is the faithful and wise servant, whom the master has put in charge of the servants in his household to give them their food at the proper time? It will be good for that servant whose master finds him doing so when he returns. Truly I tell you, he will put him in charge of all his possessions. But suppose that servant is wicked and says to himself, 'My master is staying away a long time,' and he then begins to beat his fellow servants and to eat and drink with drunkards. The master of that servant will come on a day when he does not expect him and at an hour he is not aware of. He will cut him to pieces and assign him a place with the hypocrites, where there will be weeping and gnashing of teeth."

Parable of the Rich Fool
Luke 12:13-21

Someone in the crowd said to him, "Teacher, tell my brother to divide the inheritance with me."

Jesus replied, "Man, who appointed me a judge or an arbiter between you?" Then he said to them, "Watch out! Be on your guard against all kinds of greed; life does not consist in an abundance of possessions."

And he told them this parable: "The ground of a certain rich man yielded an abundant harvest. He thought to himself, 'What shall I do? I have no place to store my crops.'

"Then he said, 'This is what I'll do. I will tear down my barns and build bigger ones, and there I will store my surplus grain.' And I'll say to myself, "You have plenty of grain laid up for many years. Take life easy; eat, drink and be merry.""

"But God said to him, 'You fool! This very night your life will be demanded from you. Then who will get what you have prepared for yourself?'

"This is how it will be with whoever stores up things for themselves but is not rich toward God."

Jesus reminds us that one day we will stand face to face with God and must account for what we did with our possessions on earth. We cannot take them with us. Understanding ourselves as eternal souls who cannot take our possessions with us should change how we think about what we do. It, in fact, reverses the typical question asked about the "Spark Tank" family. People hear about the gift of half a million dollars and think, "Who would do such a thing? What amazing faith they must have!" As I know this anonymous family well, I can attest that they have a deep and powerful faith, but with these scriptures in mind, it raises a different question for all the rest of us: "If we believe we will one day be face to face with God, giving an accounting of what we have done with our resources, who would *not* do such a thing?"

Jesus's parables about heaven are like a coach making sure that we have leveraged everything we have while we still have the time to do it! The owner comes back to see whether the servant has been faithful even though the owner has been away. God says to the rich man, why simply store up goods? Can you take them with you?

One of my professors at seminary, Richard Hays, believed deeply that this was one of the critical questions that Jesus asks repeatedly in Scripture. He would often be asked to teach on controversial topics in the life of the church, but he preferred to preach on wealth. Jesus spoke far more often about money than he did on any of the other "hot topic" issues in the church. Most of Hays's teaching and lectures took place before smart phones and budgeting apps when people carried check books and when the transactions were recorded on the back page of the check book. He said the best way to understand Jesus's comments on this was to pull out the page that marked down how much and where you had been spending your resources, and hand it to the person sitting next to you. Then have a conversation about whether your transactions match your faith. Most people would not want to have that conversation.

Jesus tells us that we will all have that conversation with God. Christians believe that we are saved by faith, but that our faith must be reflected in what we do with all that God has given us. All. Not just ten percent.

Don't Stop At The Tithe

Why did God create the world? All the beauty and diversity that we see around us—why is it here? It is here because of love. God existed before the universe and created it out of nothing. God made creatures that walk on the ground, that fly in the air, and swim in the sea, and then God made us. God gave us the entire world and asked us to take care of it. Even when we broke it, God gave us more. God gave us God's own self: "This is how God showed his love among us: He sent his one and only Son into the world that we might live through him" (1 John 4:9).

God made the world and gave everything for us. In our relationship with God, God wants us to give God everything in return. Like a marriage, where the husband gives all for the wife and the wife gives all for the husband, so God gave us everything, and we give everything back.

In the Old Testament—the first part of the Bible before Jesus entered the world at Christmas—giving a *tithe* back to God was the expectation of Noah, Abraham, and the Jewish people. The *tithe*—ten percent of what we earned, or grew, or shepherded—was to be given back to God. Jesus came and, through his teachings, helped us to understand that our money and resources are often a proxy for understanding our heart. In the "Sermon on the Mount," Jesus says, "No one can serve two masters. Either you will hate the one and love the other, or you will be devoted to the one and despise the other. You cannot serve both God and money" (Matthew 6:24).

When we talk about money in church, we often rely on the Old Testament standard of the tithe. To be clear, I believe in the tithe, but I believe the tithe is only a starting point. Many think that the only biblical mandate is to give ten percent and that we get to do whatever we wish with the other ninety percent. But Jesus never said this. Instead, he said that we are either going to serve God or money. Jesus said we would be held to account for *all* that God has given us. He told parables about whether we leveraged everything to God. John Wesley said it this way:

> "Render unto God," not a tenth, not a third, not half, but all that is God's, be it more or less; by employing all on yourself, your household, the household of faith, and all mankind, in such a manner, that you may give a good account of your stewardship when ye can be no longer stewards.[8]

The tithe is simply a minimum. Once we have given ten percent to the church, then we look at everything we have and ask, how can we leverage this for heaven? If you pay a mortgage or rent for an apartment or house, how do you use the space that God has given you for community? If you pay for groceries and are cooking dinner, who needs food and good conversation? If you have plenty, how can you take it and use it for a better world?

This is what solid souls do. They look at their gifts, their resources, and their community, and they find ways to transform the world. Solid souls are not worried about being confronted by God when they die. They are thrilled to show God how they have taken what God has given them and made even more out of it.

Shriveled souls, on the other hand, choose something other than God—their reputations, careers, or assets—and put their heart into those things. In the end, those things mean very little. None of that can go with you to heaven. In Charles Dickens's classic tale, *A Christmas Carol*, Ebenezer Scrooge counted assets. His heart resided with his money rather than his family or his clerk Bob Cratchit and Bob's son Tiny Tim.

Like Ebenezer Scrooge in Dickens's brilliant story, we have the opportunity today to see the world differently, to choose to have our hearts bound up with the love of God and the love of our neighbor. We can have great careers and reputations and even a lot of assets and still be faithful to God as long as those assets are leveraged in such a way that we can stand before God and be proud that we used everything, not just ten percent, for a better world.

Live Whole, Resource Heaven

The greatest gift the "Spark Tank" family gave St. Andrew was what came with the gift of half a million dollars. It was the gift of seeing a new way to understand faith and the role of a church. Most of my life, I had been looking at the institution of the church and wondering how a congregation could come up with an ever-bigger project. Instead, I saw how many different projects came out of people's imaginations. My job as a pastor was not simply to come up with ideas that people could participate in, but to spark the imagination of what each of us could do if we all saw the world and asked, what can I do to live my whole life for God?

I have seen in my life and the life of others that, when we live out of that question, we become better versions of ourselves. Our very being becomes stronger and more solid. The very concept of a solid soul is one where every part of our life becomes a virtuous cycle of loving God and loving others. This is what I want in my relationship with my children, my marriage to my wife, the people at my church, the children at neighborhood schools—everybody!

Shriveled souls choose a lesser question, one about greed, or selfishness, or pride; over time, their impact and vision become smaller. They focus on themselves and not God or others. I do not want that for my own life, and I don't want it for yours. God doesn't want that either.

In these pages, I have tried to tell stories that inspire and create a vision for a different life. Stories about my grandfather Bill Reece, David Michel, and Epiphanie are about people who chose to invest their lives on earth in a way that made a difference for others.

This is what we can do when we take the limited time we have here on earth and our limited resources and ask, where can I use all that God has given me to create a new and better world? What we discover when we ask this question is that we become more solid souls, souls who can help others become more solid souls.

If you feel like your faith has become irrelevant or dull, try to make someone's life better. You don't need matching funds from a "Spark Tank" family to leverage the choices you make for heaven. You are an eternal soul of infinite value. You too have something special to give.

Leave it all out on the field. Use everything you are to bring about heaven, then see if you don't find your faith coming alive and yourself as a more solid soul.

Epilogue

A Paraphrase Of Lewis's Preface To *The Great Divorce*

I believe that Lewis's preface to *The Great Divorce* is the greatest few pages he has ever written. I also believe that it is inaccessible to most people. When people read that book, I tell them to read the preface, read the book, and then return to the preface to see if it makes sense. As a part of this process, I decided to attempt a rewrite of that preface in order to provide another lens for people to access it. Much like Eugene Peterson's *The Message*, which is a paraphrase of the Bible, this is a paraphrase of Lewis. To be clear, I do not believe that this work supplants his original genius, but rather I offer another lens to approach the fundamental truth that has changed my life.

William Blake wrote the *Marriage of Heaven and Hell*. Lewis wrote of their divorce. In some sense or other, these two approaches to the world are engaged in every conversation, relationship, and decision of our lives. Blake's approach is part of a persistent attempt to claim that the consequences of our decisions are not actually realized in the end. If heaven and hell are merged, then what does it matter what we believe or what we do? In time, everything will end up okay without any drastic effort on our part.

But if heaven and hell are divorced, then we must choose one path over another. We cannot be faithful in a marriage *and* commit adultery. Jesus says it this way:

> You have heard that it was said, 'You shall not commit adultery.' But I tell you that anyone who looks at a woman lustfully has already committed adultery with her in his heart. If your right eye causes you to stumble, gouge it out and throw it away. It is better for you to lose one part of

your body than for your whole body to be thrown into hell. And if your right hand causes you to stumble, cut it off and throw it away. It is better for you to lose one part of your body than for your whole body to go into hell (Matthew 5:27-30).

To have a good marriage, you have to reject the single life. This is true for every decision that we make from the time that we are born. If a child chooses to play competitive soccer, he or she must say no to football. If we choose to be kind to our family, we must not speak poorly of them behind their backs. In fact, every decision we make necessitates saying no to something else. This then brings us to another place where we have to make a new decision. The basic structure of our world is like that. Whales and dolphins became sea creatures, which means that they are not able to climb trees. An orca and a gorilla are vastly different from each other. Even good things are different from one another. This rejection is even more clear in our choices between what is bad and what is good.

The desire to say that choices don't matter comes from a good place, but that thought takes away the incentive for someone to reject hell. This is exactly the wrong way to help those who choose bad pathways in their life. Telling them that choices don't matter keeps them in their hell. Bad choices do not have to define us for eternity, but they require turning back the other way. It is like an algebra equation. If you make a mistake on a single math problem, it can be fixed, but you have to go backward in the logic in order to find where you made the mistake, and then correct it. If you have made a mistake and decide to keep going, it will never become right.

This is how it is with our souls. We can redeem our bad choices but not by continuing to make bad choices in the hope that somehow this time it will be right. Life is still an either/or choice. If we persist on the road of poor choices, we will not see the results of good choices. Because we are souls, this should be seen from an eternal viewpoint. If we insist on staying in hell, we won't see heaven. If we wish to experience heaven, we must say no to anything that isn't good.

That rejection, though, is harsher than it sounds, because in heaven all things will be made right. If you did as Jesus suggested and actually plucked out your right eye, in heaven you would find that in the end of all things, you would be able to see again. All of the things that we must reject on earth, greed, selfishness, pride, lust, and envy, will be found redeemed in heaven. In fact, our core desires will be fulfilled even more fully in heaven.

The desire to merge heaven and hell is to say that all things will be fine in the end. This is true. In heaven, everything wrong will be made right. In this way, when you get to heaven, you will see—for those who have made the choice—that everything bad in their lives has been redeemed. Alcoholism, for instance, will be dignified in heaven for those who have taken a different path, one of recovery and redemption. But on this side of heaven, we cannot say that alcoholism is good. If we say that, then we are likely to hurt people who are in the throes of alcoholism and have not yet reached their final healing. We don't want to embrace the concept that our decisions and choices do not matter, saying that everything is good and no choice results in a real hell.

On this side of death, we cannot imagine how we will see the present once earth and heaven become renewed. It would be like a parent explaining to one child that they will love their second child just as much. Or it would be like explaining how a breakup can be a learning and growing thing to a youth in the throes of his or her first love. We cannot say that all things are good, even if, through the process of redemption, they can become good, because for souls on this side of eternity, the choice of heaven and hell is still before us.

So how should we imagine our time on earth? How we remember our lives on earth will depend greatly on whether we—in the end—choose heaven or hell. Just as a divorce contaminates the marriage that came before it, hell—if chosen instead of heaven—will poison even the good that we experience right now. We think that hell or heaven are triggered by death, but we will know that is not true in the end. Heaven will mean a redemption of even the worst parts of the earth, making it seem as if our time on earth was simply the first season in the eternity of heaven.

What lies before us is still our choice. Because we are eternal souls, we make the choice of either a solid existence in heaven or a shriveled existence in hell each and every moment.

Endnotes

Introduction: Solidify Your Soul

[1] "Soul Has Weight, Physician Thinks," *New York Times* special report (March 11, 1907), https://www.nytimes.com/1907/03/11/archives/soul-has-weight-physician-thinks-dr-macdougall-of-haverhill-tells.html.

[2] "21 grams experiment," *Wikipedia*, last modified January 19, 2021, 01:25, https://en.wikipedia.org/wiki/21_grams_experiment.

[3] The Charlie Daniel's Band, "The Devil Went Down to Georgia," Charles Fred Hayward, et al., writers, © Songs Of Universal Inc. (1979).

[4] C. S. Lewis, *The Weight of Glory* (New York: HarperOne, 2001), 46.

Part One | It's All About Soul

Chapter 1: Choose To Be Whole

[1] "Inquiry on Corruption in Paving Industry Widening," *New York Times* (January 3, 1982), https://www.nytimes com/1982/01/03/us/inquiry-on-corruption-in-paving-industry-widening.html.

[2] Raymundo Perez, "Construction Firms Indicted for Bid Rigging," United Press International (November 20, 1981), https://www.upi.com/Archives/1981/11/20/Construction-firms-indicted-for-bid-rigging/6014375080400/.

[3] Perez, "Construction Firms Indicted."

[4] "Remembering John Glenn," hosted by Steve Inskeep, *Morning Edition* on NPR (December 9, 2016), https://www.npr.org/2016/12/09/504930256/remembering-john-glenn.

5 Paula Maynard, "Three Kansas Roadbuilders, Including an Elderly Dodge City Contractor…," *United Press International* (March 15, 1982), https://www.upi.com/Archives/1982/03/15/Three-Kansas-roadbuilders-including-an-elderly-Dodge-City-contractor/7932385016400/.

6 *The Good Place*, season 2, episode 5, "The Trolley Problem," directed by Dean Holland, featuring Kristen Bell and William Jackson Harper, aired October 19, 2017, on NBC, https://www.imdb.com/title/tt6951978/.

7 *The Dark Knight*, directed by Christopher Nolan, featuring Christian Bale, Michael Caine, and Heath Ledger (Warner Brothers, 2008), 152 minutes, https://www.amazon.com/Dark-Knight-Christian-Bale/dp/B001I189MQ.

8 *Sweet Magnolias*, season 1, episode 4,"Lay It All Down," directed by Kelli Williams, featuring JoAnna Garcia and Brooke Elliott, aired May 19, 2020, on Netflix.

9 Maynard, "Three Kansas Roadbuilders."

Chapter 2: Heaven (Or Hell) Begins Now

1 Andrew D. Parker, *Revelation: Revealing Ancient Understandings* (Bloomington, IN: WestBow Press, 2017), 363.

2 Laurie Santos, "The Unhappy Millionaire," in *The Happiness Lab*, podcast, season 1, episode 2, 3:40–4:18, https://www.happinesslab.fm/season-1-episodes/the-unhappy-millionaire.

3 See the Social Security Administration's "Actuarial Life Table" as of 2016 at https://www.ssa.gov/OACT/STATS/table4c6.html.

4 C. S. Lewis, *The Great Divorce* (New York, NY: MacMillan Publishing Co., 1946), 21.

5 Justin Furstenfeld, "James," on *Argue with a Tree*, by Blue October, recorded live June 4, 2004 at Lakewood Theater, Dallas, TX, CD 2, 6:13.

6 Furstenfeld, "James," introduction.

7 Justin Furstenfeld (@blueoctoberband), "Over 20 years ago I wrote a song called James. The song was a dark piece about hateful revenge and jealousy," Instagram, January 25, 2021, https://www.instagram.com/blueoctoberband/?hl=en.

Chapter 3: Shriveled Souls

1 Dr. Seuss, *How the Grinch Stole Christmas* (New York, NY: Random House, 1957), 3.

2 C. S. Lewis, *The Weight of Glory* (New York, NY: HarperOne, 1949), 26.

3 "My Shot," in *Hamilton*, Broadway musical, 2015, lyrics, https://www.themusicallyrics.com/h/351-hamilton-the-musical-lyrics/3704-my-shot-lyrics-hamilton.html.

4 The "empowerment dynamic" presents an alternative course to the "dreaded drama triangle." In this framework, the triangle is flipped, and the negative roles in the DDT now build up rather than tear down. The persecutor is now a challenger, the rescuer is now a coach, and the victim is now a creator. This is a virtuous cycle where the drama is taken away and the possibilities are endless. See David Emerald, *The Power of TED*: The Empowerment Dynamic* (Edinburgh, Scotland: Polaris, 2005).

5 "The Drama Triangle," *TED*: The Empowerment Dynamic,* accessed January 22, 2021, https://powerofted.com/drama-triangle/.

6 C. S. Lewis, *The Great Divorce* (New York, NY: MacMillan Publishing Co., 1946), 31–32.

7 Matt Jenson, *The Gravity of Sin: Augustine, Luther and Barth on 'Homo Incurvatus in Se'* (New York: T&T Clark, 2006), 6.

8 Augustine, *The Confessions of Saint Augustine,* https://www.gutenberg.org/files/3296/3296-h/3296-h.htm.

Part Two | Souls In Relationship

Chapter 4: Strengthen Your Marriage

[1] Jenny Gomez, conversation with author, November 1, 2020. Used by permission.

[2] Gary Coiro, "Burn the Ships—Cortez Allows for No Turning Back," *ServantNetwork's Blog* (blog), August 15, 2013, https:// servantnetwork.wordpress.com/2013/08/15/burn-the-ships-cortez-allows-for-no-turning-back.

[3] See Timothy Keller, with Kathy Keller, *The Meaning of Marriage* (New York, NY: Riverhead, 2011); John Gottman, *The Seven Principles for Making Marriage Work* (New York, NY: Harmony, 2015).

[4] Gottman, *The Seven Principles*, 40.

[5] Gottman, *The Seven Principles*, 11.

[6] Gottman, *The Seven Principles*, 23.

[7] See Genesis 50:20. In the biblical story that concludes Genesis and sets up Exodus, Joseph is sold off to slavery in Egypt by his older brothers. This sets off a series of ups and downs for Joseph until he ascends to the second highest rank in the country of Egypt and saves the entire region from starvation. Unknown to both Joseph and his brothers, God ended up saving the Israelite people through the evil intended by Joseph's brothers. *What you intended for bad, God has worked for good* is a paraphrase of Genesis 50:20.

[8] Gottman, *The Seven Principles*, 3.

[9] C. S. Lewis, *The Great Divorce*, preface, viii, italic original.

[10] Gottman, *The Seven Principles*, 26-36.

[11] Gottman, *The Seven Principles*, 26.

[12] Gottman, *The Seven Principles*, 80.

Chapter 5: Full-Sized Souls

[1] Kim Meyers email correspondence with the author, November 5, 2020. Used by permission.

2 Kim Meyers email correspondence.

3 Rebecca Kennedy (Dr. Becky), "Connect, Don't Fix," *Try This at Home* (blog), June 4, 2020, https://goodinside.com/blog/connect-dont-fix/.

4 Follow @drbeckyathome on Instagram.

5 Foster Cline and Jim Fay, *Parenting with Love and Logic* (Colorado Springs, CO: NavPress, 2020).

6 Kim Meyers email correspondence with the author, December 15, 2020. Used by permission.

Chapter 6: Love ≠ Sex

1 *Friends*, season 4, episode 17, "The One with the Free Porn," directed by Michael Lembeck, featuring Matt LeBlanc and Matthew Perry, aired March 26, 1998, on NBC, Netflix.

2 *Friends*, "The One with the Free Porn," script accessed at friends-tv.org/zz417.html.

3 Alexia Fernandez, "Rob Reiner Says Harry and Sally Were Not Supposed to End Up Together in When Harry Met Sally," *People* (July 15, 2019), https://www.yahoo.com/entertainment/rob-reiner-says-harry-sally-203911822.html.

4 L. Gregory Jones, "Discovering Hope Through Holy Friendships," *Faith and Leadership* (June 18, 2012), https://faithand-leadership.com/l-gregory-jones-discovering-hope-through-holy-friendships.

Chapter 7: Truth Will Set You Free

1 Reese's stories and quotations here and throughout are used with his gracious permission.

2 C. S. Lewis, *The Weight of Glory* (New York: HarperOne, 2001), 46.

3 "post-truth," Word of the Year 2016, https://languages.oup.com/word-of-the-year/2016/.

[4] Martin Gurri, *The Revolt of the Public and the Crisis of Authority in the New Millennium* (San Francisco, CA: Stripe Press, 2018), 395, italics original.

[5] See T. C. Tompkins and K. Rhodes, "Groupthink and the Ladder of Inference: Increasing Effective Decision Making," *The Journal of Human Resource and Adult Learning* 8, no. 2 (2012): 84.

[6] Stephen R. Covey, A. Roger Merrill, and Rebecca R. Merrill, *First Things First* (New York: Free Press, 1994), §2, pp. 75–188.

[7] Reese Popst interview with the author, November 2, 2020. Used by permission.

Part Three: Souls Onward And Upward

[1] David Brooks, *The Second Mountain: The Quest for a Moral Life* (New York, NY: Random House, 2019), xvi.

[2] Jim Collins, *Good to Great: Why Some Companies Make the Leap . . . And Others Don't* (New York, NY: Harper Business, 2011), 12-13, 17ff.

[3] C. S. Lewis, *The Last Battle* (New York: Collier, 1956), 171.

Chapter 8: Heaven On Earth Is Possible

[1] Learn more about Zoe Ministries at https://zoemeanslife.org.

[2] Philip Gourevitch, *We Wish to Inform You That Tomorrow We Will Be Killed with Our Families* (New York, NY: Farrar, Straus and Giroux, 1998), 3.

[3] https://www.nytimes.com/1994/06/10/world/officials-told-to-avoid-calling-rwanda-killings-genocide.html.

[4] Brian Beers, "What is an Earnings Conference Call?" Investopedia, updated November 9, 2020, https://www.investopedia.com/small-business/what-is-an-earnings-conference-call/.

[5] Benjamin Hardy, *Willpower Doesn't Work: Discover the Hidden Keys to Success* (New York, NY: Hachette, 2018), 27, italics original.

6 Hardy, *Willpower Doesn't Work*, 27.

7 Martin Fritz Huber, "The Quest to Run a Sub-Four-Minute Mile at Age 40," *Outside* (May 24, 2018), https://www.outsideonline.com/2312831/quest-run-sub-four-minute-mile-age-40.

8 For more information about Zoe's Empowerment program, see their website at https://zoeempowers.org.

9 Epiphanie Mujawimana conversations with the author on a mission trip, February 2010. Stories and quotations here and throughout used with Epiphanie's gracious permission.

10 Gaston Warner email from January 29, 2021. Used by permission.

11 Hardy, *Willpower Doesn't Work*, 13, italics original.

Chapter 9: What Were You Made To Do?

1 David Michel interview with the author, September 9, 2020. Stories and quotations used throughout this chapter with David's gracious permission.

2 "Rev. Howard Thurman: He was MLK's Mentor, and his Meeting with Gandhi Changed History," *CNN Newsource*, ABC-WC PO 9, Cincinnati,, February 1, 2019, https://www.wcpo.com/news/black-history-month/rev-howard-thurman-he-was-mlks-mentor-and-his-meeting-with-gandhi-changed-history.

3 Bill Hendricks, *The Person Called You: Why You're Here, Why You Matter & What You Should Do with Your Life* (Chicago, IL: Moody, 2014).

4 Tom Rath, *StrengthsFinder 2.0* (New York, NY: Gallup Press, 2007).

5 Rath, *StrengthsFinder 2.0*.

6 "If You Can't Handle Me at My Worst," *Dictionary.com*, Memes Dictionary, https://www.dictionary.com/e/memes/if-you-cant-handle-me-at-my-worst/.

Chapter 10: Leave It All Out On The Field

1 Vince Lombardi, "What it Takes to Be Number One," http://www.vincelombardi.com/number-one.html.

2 John Wesley, "The Almost Christian," Sermon 2 in *The Sermons of John Wesley*, The Wesley Center Online, http://wesley.nnu.edu/john-wesley/the-sermons-of-john-wesley-1872-edition/sermon-2-th-almost-christian/, §2¶8, punctuation [*sic*].

3 This is the well-known question posed to those who attended John Wesley's Methodist Society groups each time they met.

4 Wesley, "The Almost Christian," §2¶1.

5 Wesley, "The Almost Christian," §2¶9, punctuation [*sic*].

6 Sanya Mansoor, "As Families Choose Between Laundry and Food, Dallas Schools Add Washer/Dryer Sets," *Dallas Morning News*, October 26, 2016, https://www.dallasnews.com/news/education/2016/10/26/as-families-choose-between-laundry-and-food-dallas-schools-add-washer-dryer-sets/.

7 "Spark Tank 2017 DISD Washers and Dryers," St. Andrew United Methodist Church, accessed January 5, 2021, https://www.standrewumc.org/stories/Spark_Tank_2017_DISD_Washers_and_Dryers.

8 John Wesley, "The Use of Money, Sermon 50, *The Sermons of John Wesley*, Wesley Center Online, http://wesley.nnu.edu/john-wesley/the-sermons-of-john-wesley-1872-edition/sermon-50-the-use-of-money/, §3¶8.